8/2000

The

Bean

Family
Pocket Guide
Fall/Winter 1999

The

Bean

Family
Pocket Guide
Fall/Winter 1999

ISBN: 1-58221-013-6
Library of Congress Catalog Card Number: 99-61593

Editor: Wendy Chia-Klesch
Designers: Heather Ealey, Chris Decker and Kevin Gilbert
Copy Editor: Sandra Holcombe
Production Assistants: Marshall McClure and Barbara Woerner

Printed in the United States of America
To order additional copies of this book,
or to obtain a free catalog, please contact:

Antique Trader Books
P.O. Box 1050
Dubuque, IA 52004
or call
1-800-3234-7165

Dedication

This book is dedicated to my husband and daughter, who remind me that collecting bean bags should be fun—and help me keep it that way.

Acknowledgments

For their continuous support and encouragement, I thank my family and friends. Special thanks and gratitude to Tracy Crawford, Becky Fox, Dustie Meads, and Carol Williams, without whose contributions in searching for bean bags, this book would be much shorter!

Thank you to the following people for their support, feedback, and help: Tracy Anderson, Wendy Chia-Klesch, Andi Lucas, Sandra Holcombe, Allan Miller, and Elizabeth Smith.

And a whole lot of appreciation to these fine and helpful people and the companies they represent for their assistance:

Grace Añonuevo at The Idea Factory (Meanies, Star Trek Alien Beans, Spice Girl Bean Bags)
Stephanie Bennett at Tyco Preschool Toys, Inc. (Sesame Street Beans)
Judy Berwick at Gund
Adam Cohen at Liquid Blue (Grateful Dead Bean Bears)
Steven Gillman at The Limited Connection, Inc. (Classy Tassy's Bears)
Penny Gregory at Peaceable Planet (Peaceables)
Helene Guss at Russ Berrie and Company, Inc.
Kit Kiefer for Salvino's Bammers
Stephani Perlmutter at Cavanagh Group International (Coca-Cola Bean Bag Plush, Harley-Davidson Bean Bag Plush, Save the Children Bean Bags)
Kevin Ronchetto at Toy Box Creations (Veggie & Seedie Friends)
Doug Schneider at Warner Brothers
Chip Stevenson and Mela Stevens at 823 Productions (Mattel's Star Beans)

Preface

The bean bag market continues to change. No longer are collectors buying only Ty Beanie Babies. Of course, any new Beanie Baby is still a hot item, but "diversification" is the buzzword today. Collectors are buying Warner, Disney, and Coca-Cola bean bags; the new Teddy Bear lines, like Bammers and Limited Treasures; and any and all of the promotional and advertising bean bags.

As the bean bag market has changed, so has the presentation and organization of *The 1999 Bean Family Pocket Guide, Fall/Winter Edition.* In this new edition, I sought to break down the market in several key categories: Advertising and Promotional; Children's-Themed; Miscellaneous Individual and Groups; Movie-, TV-, and Music-Themed; and Sports-Related. Separate chapters are devoted to Disney Mini Bean Bag Plush, Ty Beanie Babies, and Warner Brothers Studio Store Bean Bags, and other prominent bean bag manufacturers, such as Coca-Cola, Puffkins, Gund, and Russ, are covered in their own chapter, Other Major Bean Bag Lines.

In the table of contents is a list of the bean bags in each section and the page numbers on which they can be found; in the back of the book is an overall index for all sets in all categories, making it easy to find whatever bean bag set you're looking for.

This price and identification guide chronicles nearly every bean bag issued since 1993, including more than 3,200 different listings with values, showcased in more than 600 color photos. In addition, prices are tracked for bean bags (when applicable), so you can see for yourself where the prices of your bean bags are going.

I realize there are bean bags that I haven't learned of yet and that more will be released and created between the time that I write this and the time you are reading it. I welcome you to write to me about bean bags that you feel should be included in this book, and to let me know what you think of *The Bean Family Pocket Guide.*

Enjoy the book and have a great collecting year!

Shawn Brecka
Bean Family
P.O. Box 441
Plover, WI 54467

Table of Contents

Introduction

About this Guide

The 1999 Bean Family Pocket Guide, Fall/Winter Edition has been designed as a portable, easy-to-tote reference source and price guide you can take along when you go hunting for bean bags. It has detailed lists of the most popular bean bags collectors are looking for, and values current as of mid-summer, 1999. Please remember that the lists of bean bags, their values, and retirement status are current as of 7/15/99, and new bean bags may have been issued and new retirements announced since then.

You can also use this guide to help you track trends in prices, as two prices are listed for many of the bean bags: one for the winter of 1998 (W/1998) and one for the summer of 1999 (S/1999). The Beanie Baby section has three prices, tracking values from summer of 1998 (S/1998). I think you will find this guide an immensely valuable tool in your collecting pursuits.

1999 Bean Bag Trends

There are trends galore for the second half of 1999 and beyond:

Trend #1: Bears. Teddy Bears are king in the bean bag world. There is a forest full of bears from Ty, Bammers, Celebrity Bears, Sally Winey, Limited Treasures, and others. This bean-bag bear approach is great because bean bag collectors love Teddy Bears, and, since there are many folks who collect Teddy Bears exclusively, they are buying all the Teddy Bear bean bags they can find.

Trend #2: International interest. Bean bags are a distinctly American collectible with growing worldwide appeal. Ty has issued three foreign-exclusive Teddy Bears (Brittania, Germania, and Maple); and Disney has issued several Japan-, France- and England-exclusive bean bags. Of all foreign countries, Australia seems to be leading the way in the production of bean bags, with its large set of Beanie Kids. Canada seems as bean crazy as the United States. Will Europe and Japan follow suit?

Trend #3: Collectors migrate away from Ty. There appears to be a continuing shift in collector focus away from Beanie Babies and toward other lines. It's probably due to the following factors: poor distribution, a drop in secondary market prices, overproduction, and stiff competition from other bean bag makers. With that said, I suspect Ty will bounce back with several innovative ideas that will reinvigorate its line.

Trend #4: Lower production numbers. How many bean bags a company makes is now foremost in the minds of many collectors. This is an important area for manufacturers to address. Overproduction means little secondary market interest, which can lead to collector apathy.

Trend #5: Promotional and advertising bean bags. As you can see in this guide, there's been an explosion in promo and advertising bean bags. This is currently one of the hottest segments of the market, and it will likely continue to be for years to come.

Trend #6: Celebrity, sports, and media-star bean bags. KISS, The Spice Girls, sports heroes, and country singers—and the bean bags that aren't openly marketed as "celebrities," but everyone can figure out who they're supposed to be (i.e., Celebrity Bears and others). I expect to see this area be one of the largest growing hobby segments over the next several years.

Tips for Buying & Selling Bean Bags

Buying bean bags: This is an easy thing and a tough thing. It's easy when you can find the new bean bags you want for retail price. It's tough if you can't. Seriously, though, start at the retail level, whether it's at a Beanie Baby retailer, Disney venue, Warner Brothers Studio Store, gift shop, etc., to find the bean bag you're looking for.

Retired, discontinued, and regional bean bags are another matter. Many times, if I haven't been gotten a particular bean bag through the usual retail means, I've acquired them from other collectors or dealers from across the country, and even as far away as Japan, England, and Australia. I've done most of my buying via the Internet. Bean bag shows are also great places to find items for your collection. Magazines, such as Toy Trader and Beans & Bears!, have many classified ads for bean bags, too. In some communities, clubs have been formed for members to buy, sell, and trade amongst themselves. You'll probably use all of these sources from time to time to help expand your collection.

Selling bean bags: All of the above venues can be used to sell bean bags. If you're selling bean bags in person, the sale is pretty straight- forward. If you're selling through the mail, make sure you describe the bean bag with complete accuracy. If the tag has a scratch, crease, or bend, let the buyer know that up front. If you're selling bean bags to a dealer, expect offers anywhere from 25% to 75% of the values quoted in pricing guides. Obviously, selling bean bags yourself—where you become the "dealer," is the best way to get the best price. Becoming a part-time bean bag seller, to help supplement your pocketbook for collecting, has become a lot easier with the advent of the Internet.

Buying on the Internet: I've had very few problems buying bean bags on the Internet. I'm sure you've heard stories about buyers getting ripped off through Internet dealings. Yes, scams have been pulled on people, but there are ways to protect yourself when buying online. I've purchased bean bags from individuals, companies, and through on-line auctions. If buying from an individual or company, check their references. Don't give out your credit card number unless you're 100% positive of the legitimacy of the seller, and then only through a secure server (one that makes it virtually impossible for others to tap into your message and swipe your credit card number). If the seller accepts credit cards, it's just as simple to make a phone call to place your order. One of the hottest auction sites on the Internet for buying and selling bean bags is the eBay on-line auction at:

http://www.ebay.com

Whether buying or selling as part of any on-line auction, don't jump in with both feet. Explore a bit, and take some time to become familiar with the terminology and procedures before conducting transactions online.

Learn the Lingo

Following is a list of commonly used terms and abbreviations that are specific to the bean bag collecting hobby.

Terms

American Trio: Beanie Babies Libearty, Lefty, and Righty.

Bunny Trio: Beanie Babies Hippity, Hoppity, and Floppity.

Common: A bean bag that is easily found through usual retail outlets for retail price.

Current: A bean bag that is in production and available for sale at retail stores.

Discontinued: A bean bag style or version that is no longer in production but has not been officially retired by the company.

Generation (1st, 2nd, 3rd, etc.): Refers to the style of tag used on the bean bag. Also known as "tag style."

Hang-tag: The tag that is attached to the bean bag by a plastic tag fastener or elastic (such as on the Grateful Dead Bean Bears). Typically found near the top or front of the bean bag.

Holiday bean bag: A special bean bag made for the holiday season, such as Disney's Eyeore with antlers. These bean bags are usually available only during the particular holiday season.

Limited edition: A bean bag that is produced for a certain holiday, period of time, or in limited, predetermined quantities.

Loved: Refers to a bean bag that has been played with and shows signs of wear.

Manufacturing oddity: A bean bag with an error, such as an extra leg or a missing patch, that happened during the manufacturing process.

Mistake: A bean bag with a mistake such as switched name tags.

New release: A bean bag that is the most recent new release by a company.

Promotional bean bag: A bean bag that is used to promote a company's product(s).

Rare: Often abused term to describe the availability of a bean bag. "Rare" should imply that a bean bag is hard to find because only a few exist. More often, the correct term should be "scarce." For instance, when the Beanie Baby Princess was released, it was often called "rare," but this was not true. It was hard to find not because only a few existed, but because there weren't enough to satisfy demand. It would have been more accurate to have called this bean bag "scarce."

Retired: A bean bag that is no longer in production, but may still be available at the retail level for retail price.

Scarce: Implies that a bean bag is hard to find, but there are several examples in existence. In bean-bag terms, "scarce" usually means that an item has just been released and only a small percentage of collectors/dealers have gotten their hands on the bean bag. "Scarce" bean bags usually wind up being common.

Style change: A change made to an existing bean bag resulting in a new look for the bean bag, such as a change in the material used or an item added, like a white star or black paws.

Tag protector: A plastic or acrylic device placed around or on the hang-tag to protect it.

Tush-tag: The sewn-in tag on a bean bag that usually contains manufacturing information and the like. Typically, a tush-tag is at the rear or bottom of the bean bag.

Variation: A bean bag that is a slightly different version of the bean bag initially produced. Often a small feature is changed, such as the color of the paws or a star added, to create the variation.

Abbreviations

1G, 2G, 3G, etc.: First generation, Second generation, Third generation hang-tags
BBs: Beanie Babies
CC: Credit card
CDN: Canadian
DL: Disneyland
DS: Disney Store
EX: Excellent (condition)
G: Good (condition)
HTF: Hard to find (see VHTF)
MBBP: Mini Bean Bag Plush (proper name for Disney bean bags)
MIB: Mint in bag
MIP: Mint in package
MKT: Mouseketoys
MT: Mint (condition)
MWBMT: Mint with both mint tags
MWMT: Mint with mint tags
MWT: Mint with tag (tag is not mint)
NF: New face (Beanie Baby Teddy)
NM: Near mint (condition)
NR: New release
OF: Old face (Beanie Baby Teddy)
OT: Old tag
PE: Polyethylene (type of plastic pellets used in bean bags)
PG: Price guide
PVC: Polyvinyl Chloride (type of plastic pellets used in bean bags)
(R) Retired
RET'D: Retired
S/H: Shipping and handling
TBB: Teenie Beanie Babies (McDonald's)
TBB1: 1997 Teenie Beanie Babies
TBB2: 1998 Teenie Beanie Babies
TBB3: 1999 Teenie Beanie Babies
TP: Tag Protector
TTNT: Tiny Tush Name Tag (Disney)
V1, V2, V3: Version 1, Version 2, Version 3, etc.
VG: Very good (condition)
VHTF: Very hard to find
W/: With
W/O: Without
WDW: Walt Disney World

What's In A Name?
A Note On Bean Bag Spelling

Throughout this book, you may notice that a bean's "surname" may in some instances be capitalized, and, in others, lowercased. These different spellings are used to reflect the "official" names given to the bean bags by the companies that produce them. For example, if a bean's name appears as "Blackie the Dog," then this full name is the "official" name given by the manufacturer. If it appears as "Blackie the dog," "Blackie" is the company's official name for the bean bag; "the dog" has been added solely for identification purposes.

The same principle applies to the use of beanbag vs. bean bag. Again, this book uses the same spelling the trademark owners use for their products in cases where there is a clear preference.

Different Ways to Collect

So many bean bags, so little money and little time! There are many directions you could go with your collection. Here are a few that you might find fun:

Collecting by maker: This is easy enough. Collect Beanie Babies, Puffkins, Disney, or Warner bean bags, or all the bean bags from any other maker.

Collect by animal: Birds, reptiles, farm animals, cats, bears, jungle creatures—take your pick from one or several manufacturers.

Collect by color: Do you like red or blue or green or black? Collect all the various bean bags that come in that color.

Collect by character: Do you have a favorite? Scooby, Taz, Mickey, or Pooh? Collect your critter of choice!

Collect by athlete: With so many different Mark McGwire bean bags made, a fan might try putting together a complete collection of his (or other players') bean bags.

Collect like the author: As you can see by the photos in this guide, I collect everything from the big lines to the small sets to the individual promotional bean bags. Take it from me, though, I don't suggest trying to collect everything!

Displaying & Taking Care
of Your Collection

How you display your collection is, of course, up to you. Shelves, baskets, and cases are good. If you want to keep your bean bags from everyday dust, I suggest sinking some money into a display case. The case serves to protect your bean bags from dust and cats and kids, and it is an excellent way to showcase your collection.

You can also buy individual plastic cases to hold your more valuable bean bags. These are costly (about $4 each individually or $2 each when you buy in bulk of 25 more), but they're worth it for your more expensive bean bags. For bean bags that I don't display, I pack them in air-tight plastic zipper-style bags inside plastic tubs.

And don't forget to use hang-tag protectors. There are tag protectors in every shape and size to fit just about any bean bag on the market. Protecting tags is well worth the cost, as 25% to 50% of the value of a bean bag is in the tag.

Remember that if your collection is getting especially valuable, insure it. Take pictures and keep an inventory of your collection. You can also use your camcorder to chronicle your collection. Put your photos/VCR tape and inventory list in a safety deposit box or another secure area away from your home. You never know when your collection could be stolen or lost in a natural disaster or fire. Having the visual proof of your collection will make life a lot easier if something ever happens to your collection, and you have to file an insurance claim.

About the Values in this Guide

The values for the bean bags in this guide have been arrived at through various collectors' and dealers' sales lists, Internet auction results, and input from various experts from across the United States. They are average secondary market prices for mint bean bags. This price is what you can expect to pay for a bean bag from a seller.

The values in this book should be used only as a guide. In 1999, prices for some of the bean bags in the book will increase far above the listed values, due to retirements, style changes, and other unpredictable factors. Prices for some bean bags might decrease. Keep these things in mind when using this guide.

Manufacturing mistakes: Occasionally, bean bags are produced with errors, such as one too many or too few legs, a missing tail, and so on. These errors, if legitimate, are of interest to collectors. (Some specialize in error bean bags.) There is no good way to put a value on these mutant bean bags, though. The best way to sell error versions would be at an auction.

Tag errors: Many times, hang-tags and tush-tags don't end up on the correct bean bags. Generally, these errors are not of great interest to collectors. In fact, with the proper equipment, hang-tags can easily be switched. Do not pay premium for a hang-tag error (easily faked).

Retired pieces: An (R) following a name or listing refers to a bean bag that is known to be retired.

How Condition Affects Value

Hang-Tags

Like it or not, your bean bags' hang-tags represent about 50% of their values. The tush-tags are not nearly as important as the hang-tags. It's important that the proper tush-tags are in place, but their condition has little to do with overall bean bag values. Here are some general condition factors for tags and how they affect bean bag prices:

Mint: A perfect tag without creases, scratches, dings, or dents; and no price sticker or sticker residue (if your bean bag has a price sticker, my advice is to leave it on, since you'll likely cause more damage trying to take it off). The prices in this guide are for bean bags with mint tags. As general rule, the bigger and flimsier the tag (Disney and

Warner for example), the more likely the tag is going to have some bends or creases or other problem.

Near Mint: An almost perfect tag. Often, what makes a mint tag a near mint tag is a bend, nick, or dent, but no creases. A mint tag with a price sticker on it would fall in the near mint category. Valued at 80% to 90% of the mint price.

Excellent: This tag might have a slight crease and a few other minor problems. Valued at 65% to 75% of the mint price.

Very Good: May have large creases, dents, or dings, but it is still a complete hang-tag that is displayable and pre-sentable. Valued at 50% to 60% of the mint price.

Less than Very Good: A tag with many problems, including writing on the inside or back of the tag.

These are just general guidelines, but this does make you appreciate the value of sinking a few bucks into getting the proper tag protectors. Many hang-tags will fall in between the above conditions. For instance, a perfect hang-tag with the price written on the back in marker, is not a mint tag nor is it a low-grade tag. It falls somewhere in the middle of the condition scale. Don't pay top price for a tag that is in less than top condition.

The Bean Bag

There isn't much leeway when it comes to bean bag con-dition. Either the bean bag is in mint, unplayed-with condi-tion, or it's in played-with condition. If you have mint bean bag without tags, the value is 35% to 50% that of the same bean bag with mint tags. A played-with bean bag, depend-ing on the amount of wear, could be valued from 10% to 25% of a mint bean bag with mint tags.

Another factor to consider is dirt and dust, which is espe-cially bad when it comes to light-colored bean bags. Keep the white bean bags away from dust (i.e., Seamore, Magic, Flip, etc.). Finally, sometimes the bean bags aren't mint when they arrive from the factories. Poor stitching is a com-mon complaint. If a bean bag has some factory errors, it is not considered a mint bean bag.

Counterfeit Beanie Babies®: Protect Yourself

A new market has developed for counterfeit, or "fake" Beanie Babies. So far, this doesn't seem to have happened with other brands of bean bags, but I wouldn't be surprised if particular Disney Mini Bean Bag Plush and Warner Brothers Studio Store Bean Bags had counterfeits beginning to show up. As a bean bag escalates in value, so does the desire of crooks to swindle unsuspecting consumers.

Protecting yourself is of the utmost importance, especial-ly if you are planning on paying big money for a hard-to-find retired Beanie Baby! Some things that have been noted about counterfeit beanies are poor-quality stitching, smudged or poorly printed writing on tags, and gold flaking on or uneven gold around the Ty heart hang-tag. Also, coun-terfeit "beanies" are often very under-stuffed.

Make sure that you are buying your beanies from an authorized Ty dealer (one that sells them at the suggested retail price) or a reputable secondary-market dealer. The best thing to do if you are unsure of the authenticity of a particular Beanie Baby is to compare it to one you are sure is real. Even then, it may be difficult to see the differences. As the counterfeiters become more sophisticated, it will become increasingly hard to ascertain fakes from the real thing. Here are some questions to ask when comparing an authentic Beanie Baby and a suspect Beanie:

* Look at small details, such as ears, eyes, and appendages. Are they the same shape, size, and color?
* Are the materials the same color, feel, and quality?
* Are the tush-tags the same? (Check size, ink color, smudging, spelling, and fonts used.)
* Are the hang-tags a match? (Check the gold foil, spelling, smoothness, color of ink, and fonts used.)

Great Bean Bag Resources

Throughout the book, where applicable, I have included addresses (both Internet and actual addresses) and/or phone numbers of places you can find those particular bean bags. Here are a few Internet sites that I regularly use to find out about new bean bags:

The Disney Beanie Report: http://www.dizbeanies.com
Ty official site: http://www.ty.com
Tracey's Collectibles and Gifts:
 http://members.tripod.com/~tracysgifts/collectibles.html
eBay auction site: http://www.ebay.com
Bugsbeanies: http://www.bugsbeanies.com
Scooby's Beanie Shack:
 http://looneytunes.acmecity.com/tweety/213/
BeanieMom's NetLetter: http://www.beaniemom.com
Disney Online:
 http://disney.go.com/home/homepage/today/html/index.html

advertising & promotional

A&W® Bear

1997 A&W Bear

A second version of this advertising bear was issued in 1998—this one measuring 6-1/2 inches, a half-inch taller than the first one, and with a teal hat and shirt. Both are top-quality bean bags.

Item	W/1900	S/1999
1997 A&W Bear, orange shirt and hat (R)	$12.00	$16.00
1998 A&W Bear, teal shirt and hat (R)	n/a	$8.00

AAA®

The American Automobile Association issued its own set of bean bags sporting AAA T-shirts.

Item	S/1999
Moose in red T-shirt	$6.00
Polar Bear in red T-shirt	$6.00

ABC® Ball

Available only at the New York Disney Store, this ABC Ball bean bag is a hot commodity. Reports are that it sold out quickly.

Item	S/1999
ABC Ball	$18.00

American Airlines®

A great plane and a suitcase make this an excellent set that both bean bag collectors and airline collectors vie for.

Item	W/1998	S/1999
AAiron the airplane	$38.00	$16.00
Sammy the Suitcase	n/a	$18.00

Barnum's Animals Crackers®

Nabisco issued six different animals inside boxes that resemble its famous Barnum's Animals Crackers boxes. Over the years, fifty-three different animals have been used as animal crackers (Is a set of fifty-three in the works?) This set was ordered through the Nabisco website at http://icat.nabisco.com/nabiscodirect/index.icl for $44.95.

Item	S/1999
Brown Bear	$8.00
Elephant	$8.00
Monkey	$8.00
Elephant	$8.00
Polar Bear	$8.00
Tiger	$8.00

Bell Helicopter®

Bell Helicopter (Textron) made a set of fourteen bean bags that were sold in the employee store. Each wears a bandanna, T-shirt, or tie that reads, "I'm a Hover Lover."

Item	W/1998	S/1999
Black bear	$8.00	$7.00
Brown bear	$8.00	$7.00
Brontosaurus	$8.00	$7.00
Dalmatian	$8.00	$7.00
Elephant	$8.00	$7.00
Frog	$14.00	$9.00
Hippo	$8.00	$7.00
Horse	$8.00	$7.00
Lion	$8.00	$7.00
Monkey	$8.00	$7.00
Moose	$8.00	$7.00
Pig	$8.00	$7.00
Skunk	$8.00	$7.00
Tiger	$8.00	$7.00

Best Buy®

The "Idea Box" with a Santa hat was given away to the first 100 customers on Nov. 27, 1998, at Best Buy Stores (an electronics/computer store).

Item	S/1999
Idea Box	$14.00

Biaxin®

This very cute promotional dog was offered by Abbott Laboratories as an incentive for children to finish all of their Biaxin medication. Once the medication was completed, the parent filled out a card, sent it in, and received this free Bix Bean Bag Baby.

Item	S/1999
Bix the dog	$12.00

The Big Chicken®

One of Marietta, Georgia's most famous landmarks, "The Big Chicken," a 56-foot-high, sheet-metal chicken used to advertise a local restaurant, was made in bean bag form and is really neat. The red chicken has "Kentucky Fried Chicken" and "Pepsi Cola" on its sides. This bean bag is available at The Big Chicken Restaurant in Marietta, or at Tracy's Collectibles and Gifts— online at http://members.tripod.com/~tracygifts/ (email at VannaTC@aol.com) or by writing to 864 Elmore St., Green Bay, WI 54303, (920) 498-0926, for $7.95 plus shipping. Another version of the bean bag has "The Big Chicken" on its sides and is available through the landmark's website: www.bigchicken.com

Item	S/1999
The Big Chicken	$8.00

Big Dog®

Top: Blue Shirt, Black Shirt, Red Shirt; Middle: Suction Cups, Barkman, South Bark, Sitting; Bottom: Elf, Lying Down, Barking

A set of Bean Doggies was available in 1998 from the Big Dog Sportswear catalog and at retail stores. The Big Dog Foundation is a non-profit charity that supports other charities with a focus on dogs, children, and dogs helping people. One special Big Dog bean bag was only available with a $250 catalog purchase. To request a catalog, visit Big Dog's website: http://www.bigdogs.com

Item	S/1999
Bad Dog (with black T-shirt)	$7.00
Bad Dog (with blue T-shirt)	$7.00
Bad Dog (with red T-shirt)	$7.00
Barking Dog	$8.00
Dog as Elf	$7.00
Dog Lying Down	$7.00
Dog as Santa	$15.00
Dog Sitting	$7.00
Dog w/ Suction Cups	$7.00
South Bark "Barkman"	$9.00
South Bark "Kenny"	$9.00

Blue Bunny®

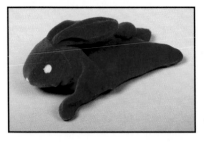

Blue Bunny, an ice cream maker, issued a bean bag of its blue bunny mascot. This bean bag can be ordered through Blue Bunny's website at http://www. bluebunny.-com/ for $5.95.

Item	S/1999
Blue Bunny	$8.00

Blue Diamond®

The Blue Diamond Company issued an almond bean bag.

Item	S/1999
Blue Diamond Almond	$12.00

Bob Evans Restaurant®

Nice set of dog bean bags from this Bob Evans Restaurant, a regional eatery.

Item	S/1999
Biscuit	$7.00
Gravy	$7.00

Borden's Elsie the Cow®

One of the better promotional bean bags around. It can be ordered online from: http://www. elsiethecow.com

Item	S/1999
Elsie the Cow	$35.00

Bubba Gump®

Bubba Gump Shrimp Co. restaurant issued a Louie the shrimp bean bag made by Fiesta. I netted Louie for $7.99 on the Bubba Gump website: http://www.bubbagump.com/index.html

Item	W/1998	S/1999
Louie the shrimp-Monterey	$10.00	$10.00
Louie the shrimp-Maui	$12.00	$12.00
Louie the shrimp-Miami	n/a	n/a

Buster Brown's Tige®

Reportedly, Tige was available as an in-store premium at Buster Brown outlets and is retired (though this could not be verified).

Item	S/1999
Tige	$15.00

Calavo®

Three hard-to-find bean bags from Calavo (California Avocado) Growers of California. Calavo has since sold out of this set.

Pinkerton Avocado

Item	S/1999
Calavo Bacon/Fuente Avacado	$15.00
Calavo Pinkerton Avocado	$15.00
Calavo Papaya	$15.00

Cap'n Crunch® Tiger Shark Meanie®

A cereal premium offer featuring a Meanie. I'm still waiting for a Cap'n Crunch "Cap'n" bean bag!

Item	S/1999
Tiger Shark Meanie	$18.00

Chef Jr. Beanbag Buddies®

The Chef Jr. Beanbag Buddies are not easy to locate on the secondary market, as collectors had to buy an enormous amount of canned food to get them. Not high quality.

Item	W/1998	S/1999
Christy the sea horse (R)	$5.00	$5.00
Jumbo the whale (R)	$5.00	$5.00
Rex the tyrannosaurus rex (R)	$5.00	$5.00
Rigatoni the dog (R)	$5.00	$5.00
Sharkeel the shark (R)	$5.00	$5.00
Steggy the stegosaurus (R)	$5.00	$5.00

Chick-Fil-A® Cow

This popular cow was a premium at Chick-Fil-A restaurants and is available at its website at http://www.chick-fil-a.com for $3.99.

Item	S/1999
Chick-Fil-A Cow	$12.00

Chuck E. Cheese®

Bean bag of the mouse mascot for Chuck E. Cheese, the children's pizza/fun and games restaurant.

Item	S/1999
Chuck E. Cheese	$7.00

CoCo Wheats® Bear

This little bean bear was a promotion through CoCo Wheats.

Item	1999
CoCo Wheats Bear	$12.00

Colgate-Palmolive® Starlight Bean Bags

Two great sets of bean bags, with a connection to the Starlight Children's Foundation. The bears were out in 1998, and the dogs were released in 1999. These were available with the purchase of Colgate-Palmolive products. Made by A&A Plush.

Item	W/1998	S/1999
Starlight Bean Bears		
Brown (R)	$5.00	$6.00
Green (R)	$5.00	$6.00
Midnight blue (R)	$5.00	$6.00
White (R)	$5.00	$6.00

Item	W/1998	S/1999
Starlight Bean Dogs		
Black	n/a	$6.00
Brown	n/a	$6.00
Tan	n/a	$6.00
White	n/a	$6.00

Copps®

The grocery chain Copps issued its own set of promotional bean bags in 1998.

Item	W/1998	S/1999
Chops the dog	$4.00	$4.00
Coco the monkey	$4.00	$4.00
I.C. the penguin	$4.00	$4.00
Inspector (man)	$4.00	$4.00
Wink the rabbit	$4.00	$4.00

Creative Memories® "Scrappie" the bear

Creative Memories, one of the leading makers of scrapbooks and supplies, has issued this cute bear named "Scrappie." Available to consultants only upon placing a qualifying order, this bear will be difficult for collectors to find. I borrowed this one from my local consultant to photograph and am considering becoming a consultant so that I can get one (just kidding!).

Item	S/1999
Scrappie	$60.00

Culver's Restaurant®

This ice cream cone mascot for Culver's Restaurant, a regional eatery, was offered as a bean bag with a key chain in his head.

Item	S/1999
Scoopie	$6.00

Dairy Queen®
Curly Top

Company mascot Curly Top is Dairy Queen's entrant into the promotional bean bag market. This bean bag stands 13 inches high!

Item	W/1998	S/1999
Curly Top	$12.00	$12.00

Diamond Crystal®

Specialty food-maker Diamond Crystal Specialty Foods, Inc., released a set of three Diamond Crystal Salt bean bags.

Item	S/1999
Cat	$9.00
Mascot with earmuffs	$9.00
Mascot with shorts	$9.00

Digital Link® Man

Mascot bean bag from the Digital Link company. Digital Link is on the Internet at: www.dl.com

Item	S/1999
Digital Link Man	$12.00

Dole® Pooka (Anastasia)

Pooka, a dog from the animated film *Anastasia* was available as a premium through Dole.

Item	W/1998	S/1999
Pooka (R)	$6.00	$6.00

Emla Cream® Drop

This bean bag resembles a drop of "Emla" cream, a pharmaceutical used as an anesthetic on the skin. I bought this one in an online auction and was told it was given to doctors as a promotion for using Emla Cream.

Item	S/1999
Emla Cream Drop	$12.00

Energizer® Bunny

This premium bunny was available in 1998, through a battery offer, as well as sold in stores such as Walgreen's. It's a very common bean bag.

Item	W/1998	S/1999
Energizer Bunny (R)	$5.00	$6.00

Entenmann's® Bean Bag Sweeties

Snack maker Entenmann's offered a set of three Bean Bag Sweeties in 1998. They were made by Bean Sprouts.

Item	W/1998	S/1999
Chip the chocolate chip cookie (R)	$9.00	$10.00
Richie the doughnut (R)	$9.00	$10.00
Sprinkles the cupcake (R)	$9.00	$10.00

Exxon® Tiger

Originally available at Exxon gas stations, now sold out.

Item	S/1999
Exxon Tiger, brown	$6.00
Exxon Tiger, gold	$6.00
Exxon Tiger, orange	$6.00
Exxon Tiger, white	$6.00

FedEx®

Generic-style animals with a FedEx (Federal Express) shirt. Available to FedEx employees.

Item	S/1999
Moose	$10.00
Monkey	$10.00

Flavorite®

Riley is a premium from Flavorite Cereal.

Item	S/1999
Riley the dog	$12.00

Frullati Café®

Rudy Frullati (the penguin) is a premium bean bag from the national chain Frullati Café.

Item	S/1999
Rudy Frullati	$10.00

General Mills®
Big G Breakfast Babies

Count Chocula, Chip, Honey Nut Bee, Lucky, Wendell, Trix Rabbit, Sonny

These General Mills cereal bean bags are popular sellers, but are available in good quantities.

Item	W/1998	S/1999
Chip the Cookie Hound (R)	$10.00	$8.00
Count Chocula (R)	$10.00	$8.00
Honey Nut Cheerios Bee (R)	$10.00	$8.00
Lucky the Leprechaun (R)	$10.00	$8.00
Sonny the Cuckoo Bird (R)	$10.00	$8.00
Trix Rabbit (R)	$10.00	$8.00
Wendell the Baker (R)	$10.00	$8.00

Girl Scouts®

Belly Beans is the name of the Girl Scout bean bags made by Mary Meyer. Two sets have come out so far, and both are excellent! An individual Girl Scouts Trefoil cookie bean bag is also available. Each is individually numbered on its hang-tag.

Girl Scout Tiny Trefoil

Top: Junior Girl Scout Dog, Cadet Girl Scout Cat; Bottom: Daisy Girl Scout Cow, Brownie Girl Scout Bear

Top: Volunteer Frog, Be Prepared Camel; Bottom: Mom Kangaroo, Make New Friends Monkey, Waggs Zebra

Item	S/1999
Belly Beans Set #1	
Brownie Girl Scout Bear	$10.00
Cadet Girl Scout Cat	$8.00
Daisy Girl Scout Cow	$8.00
Junior Girl Scout Dog	$8.00
Belly Beans Set #2	
American Panda	$15.00
Be Prepared Camel	$15.00
Make New Friends Monkey	$12.00
Mom Kangaroo	$12.00
Volunteer Frog	$9.00
Waggs Zebra	$9.00
Trefoil	
Tini Trefoil	$18.00

Gloria Jean's Coffees®

Gloria Jean's Coffees issued this excellent "coffee bean" bean bag during the 1998 holiday season for $6.

Item	S/1999
Gloria Jeanie Beanie (R)	$14.00

Godiva®

It was very difficult for me to buy this Godiva bean bag bear. I was "forced" to eat the chocolate that came with it! Ordered through the Godiva catalog in early 1999.

Item	S/1999
1999 Vaientine Bear	$16.00

Goldfish Crackers®

The Pepperidge Farm Goldfish was available through a mail-in offer for only two months in 1999.

Item	S/1999
Smiley Goldfish, rabbit ears (R)	$13.00

Goodyear® Blimp

Really neat promotional blimp. Made by AdVantage Industries.

Item	S/1999
Goodyear Blimp	$12.00

Hawaiian Punch®

Great likeness of Punchy, the colorful character promoting Hawaiian Punch. This bean bag was available from bean bag retailers.

Item	S/1999
Punchy	$10.00

Heinz®

The H.J. Heinz Company released several interesting bean bags made by the AdGap Group. "Leader of the Packets" is the coolest, with a fake leather jacket. These were offered through the Heinz Collector's Club, but Leader of the Packets is sold out and is no longer available. The Collector's Club can be contacted on the Internet through Heinz's site: http://www.heinz.com

Item	S/1999
Leader of the Packets	$16.00
Pickle	$10.00
Tomato	$10.00
Private Pickle	$10.00
Baby Dill Pickle	$10.00

Herr's Potato Chips®

This is the bean bag version of Herr's Potato Chips mascot "Chipper."

Item	S/1999
Chipper the chipmunk	$10.00

Hershey's®

Several excellent bean bags from Hershey's. Some were available through retail stores like KayBee. The Chocolate Lab was available through a premium offer.

Item	S/1999
Cow (Moo-Chelle with hat)	$8.00
Dog (Dexter with hat)	$8.00
Chocolate Lab	$12.00
Hershey's Chocolate bar	$10.00
Kiss, gold	$8.00
Kiss, green	$8.00
Kiss, red	$8.00
Kiss, silver	$8.00
Reese's Peanut Butter Cup	$18.00

Holiday Inn®

Holiday Inn and the Discovery Channel teamed up for this 1998 promotion. You had to stay overnight at Holiday Inn with your child to get just one of these bean bags.

Item	S/1999
Fezzan the lizard	$4.00
King George the penguin	$4.00
Namibia the lion	$4.00
Victoria the whale	$4.00
Virunga the gorilla	$4.00

Holsum Bread® "Bread Babies"

Sally Slice was distributed through a mail-in offer from Holsum Bread during 1998.

Item	S/1999
Sally Slice (R)	$10.00
Slugger Slice (R)	$10.00

Home Depot®

Homer the Home Depot mascot makes for a cute bean bag with his detailed clothes. It was available at Home Depot stores.

Item	S/1999
Homer (R)	$13.00

Hostess®

Buddy Butternut from Butternut Bread, Freddy the Fresh Guy from Wonder Bread, and Twinkie the Kid rode into the bean bag arena with excellent likenesses. All available from Hostess outlets in 1998.

Item	S/1999
Buddy Butternut (R)	$16.00
Freddy the Fresh Guy (R)	$20.00
Twinkie the Kid (R)	$22.00

Hush Puppies®

Set #1: Blue Bayou, Logo Basset, Salad Green, Miami Coral, Beet, Royal Purple

Set #2: Top: Berry Frappe, Chantilly; Bottom: Jet Black, Logo Bunting Blue, Logo Basset

The Applause-made Hush Puppies dog bean bag sets are some of the best ever issued. The first set was issued in 1997 and retired in July 1998; the second set was released in 1998 and retired in March 1999. A third set debuted in the spring of 1999 and was retired in July 1999. Special edition dogs were unleashed in 1999 (includ-

Set #3: Top: Lively Lilac, Cascade Blue, Meadow Mist; Bottom: Passion Pink, Spring Logo, Lemon Meringue

ing two "scented" dogs that smell like flowers), as well as at least three with tags that read, "Special Edition." Another (lying down, not sitting) was reportedly given away for buying Hush Puppy eyewear and was made by Classic Merchandising.

Item	W/1998	S/1999
Applause Set #1		
Beet (R)	$9.00	$9.00
Blue Bayou (R)	$9.00	$9.00
Logo Basset (R)	$9.00	$9.00
Miami Coral (R)	$9.00	$9.00
Royal Purple (R)	$9.00	$9.00
Salad Green (R)	$9.00	$9.00

Applause Set #2

Berry Frappe (R)	$8.00	$8.00
Bunting Blue (R)	$8.00	$8.00
Chantilly (R)	$8.00	$8.00
Jet Black (R)	$8.00	$8.00
Logo Basset (R)	$8.00	$8.00

Applause Set #3

Cascade Blue (R)	n/a	$7.00
Lemon Meringue (R)	n/a	$7.00
Lively Lilac (R)	n/a	$7.00
Meadow Mist (R)	n/a	$7.00
Spring Logo (R)	n/a	$7.00
Passion Pink (R)	n/a	$7.00

Applause Scented

Lilac, scented	n/a	$10.00
Meadow Mist, scented	n/a	$10.00

Classic Merchandising

Brown and white dog, lying down	n/a	$10.00

Intel® BunnyPeople Bean Bags

The Bunny People bean bags are based on the characters featured on the Intel television ads for Pentium II in 1998. Sporting crinkly iridescent bunny suits, they were available only at Intel employee stores for $5.99 each.

Item	W/1998	S/1999
Intel BunnyPeople, blue	$11.00	$11.00
Intel BunnyPeople, green	$11.00	$11.00
Intel BunnyPeople, pink	$11.00	$11.00
Intel BunnyPeople, purple	$11.00	$11.00
Intel BunnyPeople, yellow	$11.00	$11.00

Keebler® Elf Bean Bag

Ernie the Keebler Elf is very popular. This bean bag can be purchased through the company at its website (http://www.keebler.com) for $5.50.

Item	W/1998	S/1999
Ernie the Keebler Elf	$8.00	$9.00

Kellogg's® Cereal

Snap!, Crackle!, Pop!

Kellogg's Breakfast Bunch bean bags are all excellent to add to your collection. These were available through mail-in offers, at grocery stores, and in special promotions.

Cornelius, Toucan Sam, Dig 'Em, Tony the Tiger

Wee Beans: Tony the Tiger, Toucan Sam, Dig 'Em

Lendy Bagel, Wally Waffle

Item	W/1998	S/1999
Kellogg's Bean Bag		
Breakfast Bunch		
Cornelius	$14.00	$10.00
Crackle!	$10.00	$7.00
Dig 'Em	$12.00	$8.00
Lendy Bagel (Lender's)	n/a	$30.00
Pop!	$10.00	$7.00
Snap!	$10.00	$7.00
Tony the Tiger	$15.00	$8.00
Toucan Sam	$14.00	$8.00
Wally Waffle (Eggo)	n/a	$28.00
Kellogg's Wee Beans		
Dig 'Em	n/a	$6.00
Tony the Tiger	n/a	$6.00
Toucan Sam	n/a	$6.00

Kemper Insurance®

Reportedly, this horse bean bag with a "Kemper" kerchief was given to Kemper Insurance agents.

Item	S/1999
Kemper Insurance horse	$8.00

Kemp's®

These 1998 premium Kemp's cow bean bags are very popular. Look for another set to be released during 1999.

Item	S/1999
Berrie (R)	$12.00
Bon Bon (R)	$12.00
Chip (R)	$12.00
Milkshake (R)	$12.00

KFC's® Pokemon®

The Pokemon bean bags were available at Kentucky Fried Chicken in 1998 for $5 each.

Item	S/1999
Dratini the dragon #147	$7.00
Seel the seal #86	$7.00
Zubat the bat #41	$7.00
Vulpix the fox #37	$7.00

King 5 TV®

For its 50th anniversary, the mascot for King 5 TV in Seattle was made into bean bag form. King Mike's tag states he was designed in the 1940s by Walt Disney. Neat item!

Item	S/1999
King Mike	$18.00

Kraft® Dairy Fairy

The Kraft Dairy Fairy cow bean bag was available for buying Kraft Singles cheese products.

Item	W/1998	S/1999
Kraft Dairy Fairy (R)	$15.00	$15.00

La-Z-Boy® Raccoon Bean Bag

The La-Z-Boy Raccoon bean bag was a promotional giveaway for buying a La-Z-Boy product. Check your local La-Z-Boy seller for these, as my local store was selling them for $5.99.

Item	W/1998	S/1999
La-Z-Boy Raccoon	$12.00	$12.00

Life® Magazine

I got this dog by ordering a subscription to *Life* magazine. It was an offer in the Publisher's Clearing House mailing—but unfortunately, I didn't win millions of dollars, too.

Item	S/1999
Life Magazine dog	$9.00

Little Caesar's®

The famous "Pizza-Pizza" Little Caesar's Roman Man was an in-store promotion. You could purchase him for $5.99.

Item	S/1999
Roman Man	$7.00

Loaf 'N Jug®

The convenience store Loaf 'N Jug released a set of bean bags in 1998.

Item	S/1999
Boy milk	$8.00
Girl bread	$8.00

Luv's® Diapers Barney®

Available through a premium offer, this Gund-made Barney the Dinosaur is the same one that can be found in stores, but it does have a different hang-tag holder-string.

Item	S/1999
Luv's Diapers Barney	$6.00

M&M's® Plush Beanies

Two different M&M's Plush Beanies sets were only available at M&M's World in Las Vegas. The orange version, a promotion for the new "crispy" M&M's, is new in 1999.

Item	W/1998	S/1999
With arms and legs		
Blue	$10.00	$8.00
Green	$10.00	$8.00
Red	$10.00	$8.00
Yellow	$10.00	$8.00
Orange (with tennis shoes) n/a		$10.00
No arms and legs		
Blue	$12.00	$7.00
Green	$12.00	$7.00
Red	$12.00	$7.00
Yellow	$12.00	$7.00

Maine Potatoes

Promotional bean bag made by Toy Box Creations.

Item	S/1999
Maine Potato	$5.00

Mall of America®

Pair of excellent Teddy Bear bean bags with "Mall of America" embroidered on them. Sold as souvenirs at Minnesota's Mall of America.

Item	S/1999
Brown Teddy Bear	$9.00
Cream Teddy Bear	$9.00

McDonald's®

Grimace, Hamburglar, Ronald McDonald

Doctor Ann, Policeman Joe, The Princess, Cowboy Roy

Hamburger, Fries, Shake

The fast-food giant McDonald's now has three different sets of its own bean bags, all which can be purchased through its website: (http://www.mcdonalds.com). They are: three Floppy Dolls for $14.95; four McNugget Buddies for $22.99; and three Happy Meal Guys for $15.95. The latter two sets were issued in 1999 and are very well made.

Item	W/1998	S/1999
McDonald's Floppy Dolls		
Grimace	$9.00	$8.00
Hamburglar	$9.00	$8.00
Ronald McDonald	$9.00	$8.00
Happy Meal Guys		
Drink	n/a	$7.00
Fries	n/a	$7.00
Hamburger	n/a	$7.00

McNugget Buddies

Cowboy Roy	n/a	$7.00
Doctor Ann	n/a	$7.00
Policeman Joe	n/a	$7.00
The Princess	n/a	$7.00

Merrill Lynch® Bull

One of the finer promotional bean bags made, the Merrill Lynch Bull is very difficult to find.

Item	S/1999
Merrill Lynch Bull	$125.00

Milwaukee "Summerfest" Bean Bags

A set of seven generic bean bag souvenirs was made for Milwaukee's annual lakeshore festival in 1998. Since it's a regional set, it's probably tough to locate, but the bean bags aren't anything special.

Item	W/1998	S/1999
Brown dog	$5.00	$5.00
Cow	$5.00	$5.00
Dalmatian	$5.00	$5.00
Lion	$5.00	$5.00
Monkey	$5.00	$5.00
Panda	$5.00	$5.00
Pig	$5.00	$5.00
Polar Bear	$5.00	$5.00

Mindscape®

"Beanbag Norn" is from a CD-ROM called "Creatures," a Tamagotchi-like computer game from Mindscape Entertainment.

Item	S/1999
Beanbag Norn	$8.00

Mistic® Rain Forest Buddies

Four cute bean bags were available from Mistic Brands, Inc., for drinking Mistic Rain Forest Nectars. The offer expired on September 30, 1998.

Item	S/1999
"Jackie" the Jaguar (R)	$8.00
"Lucy" the Ladybug (R)	$8.00
"Sammy" the Spider Monkey (R)	$8.00
"Tommy" the Toucan (R)	$8.00

Musicland®

This aptly named moose was available at Musicland over the 1998 holiday season. Made by Fluffyville.

Item	S/1999
Murray X. Moose (R)	$7.00

NBC® Peacock Beany

This NBC Peacock bean bag was purchased through NBC's website (http://www.nbc.com/shop/nbcstuff/index.html) for $10. The other four bean bags were offered as employee exclusives.

Item	W/1998	S/1999
Employee Bear	n/a	$60.00
Employee Peacock (blue body)	n/a	$60.00
Employee Reindeer	n/a	$50.00
Employee Snowman	n/a	$50.00
NBC Peacock-white	$18.00	$14.00
NBC Peacock-blue	n/a	$12.00

Old Country Buffet®

The Old Country Buffet restaurant issued a bee bean bag during the 1998 holiday season.

Item	S/1999
Bee	$12.00

Oreo® Cookies

Available through a mail-in offer on Oreo Cookies packages, there are two different versions of this cute cookie bean bag, a smaller and a larger. Both sell for the same amount.

Item	S/1999
Oreo Cookie	$12.00

Oscar Mayer®

"Oscar" the Oscar Mayer Weinermobile was widely available as a premium in 1998. In addition, Dino and Scooby-Doo were available through a different offer that was not well publicized.

Item	W/1998	S/1999
Dino (R)	$9.00	$10.00
Oscar the Weinermobile (R)	$20.00	$14.00
Scooby-Doo (R)	$15.00	$16.00

Petco®

Petco, a pet food/supply retailer, issued a cat and dog set of "Pet Pals" bean bags.

Item	S/1999
Blue Mews cat	$7.00
Red Ruff dog	$7.00
Leap the frog	$7.00
Rocket the ferret	$7.00

Piggly Wiggly®

Piggly Wiggly, a regional grocery store, issued its pig mascot in bean bag form in 1999

Item	S/1999
Piggly Wiggly pig	$10.00

Pillsbury Doughboy®

This beloved advertising character was issued as a send-away through Pillsbury Bread in 1998.

Item	W/1998	S/1999
Pillsbury Doughboy (R)	$12.00	$8.00

Planet Hollywood® Bean Bags

Difficult to find if you are not within driving distance of a Planet Hollywood.

Item	W/1998	S/1999
Bubba the dinosaur	$10.00	$10.00
George the ape	$10.00	$10.00
Popcorn the elephant	n/a	$10.00

Planters' Mr. Peanut®

Mr. Peanut is a highly recognizable and popular advertising icon. Two different bean bags have been issued so far, the smaller of which is sold with a coffee cup. Available on the company's website at http://icat.nabisco.com/nabiscodi-rect/index.icl for $19.95.

Item	S/1999
Mr. Peanut, 10"	$10.00
Mr. Peanut, 6" (coffee cup)	$20.00

Prudential®

Apparently, this was an attempt at an exclamation point (!). Many feel it looks like a platypus, but interpretation is left up to the owner. This Prudential promotion was reportedly pulled for unspecified reasons (making this a hard-to-find item).

Item	S/1999
Unknown	$3.00

Rat Fink®

The creation of Ed "Big Daddy" Roth, Rat Fink was featured on model car kits, T-shirts, and many other items over the years. These officially licensed bean bags are very nice and hard to find.

Item	W/1998	S/1999
Rat Fink, gray	$15.00	$15.00
Rat Fink, green, suction cups	$15.00	$15.00

RCA® Chipper

Chipper is the puppy sidekick of the famous RCA dog Nipper. Reportedly, the Chipper bean bag was made as an employee program incentive.

Item	S/1999
Chipper	$16.00

Red Cross®

Two bean bags were created for the Red Cross and a third is due out in 1999. Disaster Dan is another bean bag available through Tracy's Collectibles and Gifts website at http://members.tripod.com/~tracygifts/ (email at VannaTC@aol.com) or by writing to 864 Elmore St., Green Bay, WI 54303, or calling (920) 498-0926.

Item	S/1999
Beara Barton, 1st Edition	$40.00
Beara Barton, 2nd Edition	n/a
Disaster Dan	$9.00

Rockford Police & Fire Chaplains

This set was produced as a fundraiser for the Rockford, Illinois, Police and Fire Chaplains. They are generic-style bean bags and probably very hard to find.

Item	S/1999
Brown dog	$6.00
Dalmatian	$6.00

Sargento® Dynamo

The mascot for Sargento cheese products, Dynamo was issued as a mail-in offer promotional bean bag in 1998.

Item	W/1998	S/1999
Dynamo (R)	$15.00	$12.00

Shell® Oil Tankers

Shell Oil Company offered this pair of oil truck bean bags on a limited basis.

Item	S/1999
Sheldon	$26.00
Shelly	$26.00

ShopRite® Supermarket

There are six neat little Teddy Bears named "Scrunchy" in this East Coast-based ShopRite Supermarket set. The purple bear was reportedly made in limited numbers.

Item	S/1999
Brown with ribbon	$7.00
Brown with T-shirt	$7.00
Purple with ribbon	$18.00
Red with ribbon	$7.00
Red with T-shirt	$7.00
Yellow with ribbon	$7.00

Smucker's® Devon & Cornwall

From the movie *Quest for Camelot*, comes this Smucker's premium Devon & Cornwall bean bag. Produced by The Idea Factory.

Item	S/1999
Devon & Cornwall	$7.00

Southwest Airlines®

Shamu, T.J. Luv

Interesting and excellent set of airplane bean bags from Southwest Airlines, available to employees only.

Item	S/1999
Lone Star	$18.00
Shamu	$16.00
T.J. Luv	$18.00

Spam®

My husband had to eat a lot of Spam so I could get this Spam Can bean bag.

Item	S/1999
Spam Can	$14.00

Starkist Tuna®
Charlie Bean Bag

Charlie is already proving to be a real favorite of bean bag collectors and those who collect Charlie the Tuna memorabilia. This was a mail-in offer.

Item	W/1998	S/1999
Charlie the Tuna (R)	$12.00	$12.00

Travelodge®

This bear was available at Travelodge hotels.

Item	S/1999
Travelodge bear	$14.00

Union Pacific Railroad®

This adorable little bear with the Union Pacific logo on its chest was available from the Union Pacific website at http://www.uprr.com/uprr/retail/ or through the company store catalog.

Item	S/1999
Union Pacific Bear white	$8.00
Union Pacific Bear red	$8.00

VFW® Buddy Poppy

Available through the VFW, Poppy is currently sold out, but more will possibly be distributed this year.

Item	S/1999
Poppy	$9.00

Walker's® 50th Birthday Bean Bear

This great-looking bear from Great Britain was produced for Walker's Crisps (potato chips) for the 50th anniversary of the company. I bought mine from a fellow collector. They are not easy to find.

Item	W/1998	S/1999
Bean Bear	$15.00	$16.00

Where's Waldo®

Waldo and Woof were available though an offer on Life cereal, which ended in 1998. Not the best-made bean bags ever produced, there is always interest on the secondary market.

Item	W/1998	S/1999
Waldo (R)	$9.00	$12.00
Woof the dog (R)	$9.00	$12.00

Children's
Themed

Anne Geddes®

These bean bags were inspired by the creations of baby photographer Anne Geddes. They are available in combinations including: dark or light skin, mouth open or closed, and eyes open or closed. The only place I've seen them is at Target stores.

Item	S/1999
Baby Bears (any style)	$8.00
Baby Bunnies (any style)	$9.00
Baby Butterflies (any style)	$10.00
Baby Ladybugs (any style)	$8.00

Crayola®

This is the only Crayola bean bag I've located, though I would guess there may be others.

Item	S/1999
Crayola Crayon	$10.00

Crocodile Creek®

From the children's book, *Guess How Much I Love You*, comes a Little Nutbrown Hare bean bag. He was sold wherever the book was sold.

Item	W/1998	S/1999
Little Nutbrown Hare	$8.00	$8.00

Curious George®

Several bean bags have been issued for this long-time children's storybook favorite.

Item	W/1998	S/1999
Gund Curious George (9-1/2")	$12.00	$10.00
Curious George in Radio Flyer Wagon	$15.00	$12.00
Equity Toys		
Curious George, Big Yellow Hat	n/a	$9.00
Curious George, Fishing	n/a	$8.00
Curious George, Pajamas	n/a	$7.00
Curious George, Space Suit	n/a	$7.00

Dr. Seuss®

Characters from Dr. Seuss books have been made into bean bags. The Mattel set is from 1997 and was sold in display boxes. The Dayton's "Max" bean bag was reportedly distributed for one day only —on the day after Christmas, 1998.

Front: Thidwick the Moose;
Back: Yertle the Turtle, The Cat in the Hat, Horton the Elephant

Item	W/1998	S/1999
Dayton's		
Max (Grinch's dog)	n/a	$40.00
Mattel		
The Cat in the Hat	$10.00	$10.00
Horton the Elephant	$10.00	$10.00
Thidwick the Moose	$10.00	$10.00
Yertle the Turtle	$10.00	$10.00

Furby Buddies®

Riding on the coattails of the hottest holiday toy of 1998, Tiger Electronics followed up with a set of twenty-four Furby bean bags that mimicked the real Furbys in appearance. The bean bags are of excellent quality.

Top: "Big Light," "Up Down," "Very Good";
Bottom: "Love Me," "Big Dance," "More Light"

Item	S/1999
Black, blue eyes, "Good Pet"	$10.00
Black, brown eyes, "No Hungry"	$8.00
Black, gray eyes, "Very Hungry"	$9.00
Black, green eyes, "Big Light"	$8.00
Black & white, blue eyes, "Very Good"	$9.00
Black & white, brown eyes, "Sleep Good"	$7.00
Black & white, gray eyes, "Good Joke"	$8.00
Black & white, green eyes, "Light Please"	$7.00
Gray, blue eyes, "Up Down"	$6.00
Gray, brown eyes, "More Happy"	$6.00
Gray, gray eyes, "Like Joke"	$9.00
Gray, green eyes, "Done Sleep"	$8.00
Gray & pink, blue eyes, "No Worry"	$9.00

Gray & pink, brown eyes, "Sleep More"	$8.00
Gray & pink, gray eyes, "More Light"	$9.00
Gray & pink, green eyes, "More Hug"	$10.00
Gray & white, blue eyes, "Hug Me"	$7.00
Gray & white, brown eyes, "Love Me"	$7.00
Gray & white, gray eyes, "More Please"	$7.00
Gray & white, green eyes, "Like Up"	$7.00
White, blue eyes, "Big Dance"	$10.00
White, brown eyes, "Love Hug"	$8.00
White, gray eyes, "Big Hug"	$8.00
White, green eyes, "Good Sleep"	$10.00

Garfield® Bean Bags

Front: Garfield, Nermal, Odie;
Back: Arlene, Pooky

High quality set of this famous cartoon feline and friends. These are available in the "Garfield Stuff" catalog (888-374-PAWS) or online (http://www.catalog.garfield.com). And if you're a Garfield enthusiast, be sure to check out the main Garfield website at: http://www.garfield.com

Item	W/1998	S/1999
Arlene	$8.00	$7.00
Garfield	$8.00	$7.00
Nermal	$8.00	$7.00
Odie	$8.00	$7.00
Pooky	$8.00	$7.00

Mother Goose's Bean Bag Friends®

Sold exclusively at Target Stores, this is an excellent set to acquire. Produced by Commonwealth, the hang-tag includes the Mother Goose rhyme for each character.

Front: Hickory Dickory Dock, Baa Baa Black Sheep, Cat and the Fiddle; Back: Humpty Dumpty, Cow Jumped Over the Moon

Item	S/1999
Baa Baa Black Sheep	$6.00
Cat and the Fiddle	$6.00
Cow Jumped Over the Moon	$6.00
Hickory Dickory Dock	$6.00
Humpty Dumpty	$8.00

My Little Pony® Bean Bags

The famous children's My Little Pony characters were made as bean bags by Hasbro in 1998. They do not seem to have had wide distribution.

Sky Skimmer, Dainty Dove, Sweet Berry, Sundance, Ivy, Light Heart

Item	W/1998	S/1999
Dainty Dove	$9.00	$10.00
Ivy	$9.00	$10.00
Light Heart	$9.00	$10.00
Sky Skimmer	$9.00	$10.00
Sundance	$9.00	$10.00
Sweet Berry	$9.00	$10.00

Paddington Bear®

The children's character Paddington Bear was made into two bean bags in 1998 by Kid's Gifts. This set was purchased at a Sears store.

Item	W/1998	S/1999
Paddington, blue coat	$6.00	$7.00
Paddington, red coat	$6.00	$7.00

PEANUTS® Bean Bags

So far, there have been three different sets based on the PEANUTS cartoon strip. By the listings below, you can see how big a draw Snoopy is!

Item	W/1998	S/1999
PEANUTS Collection, Kohl's (Applause)		
Charlie in Santa hat	n/a	$7.00
Snoopy as Flying Ace	n/a	$7.00
Snoopy as Joe Cool	n/a	$7.00

Snoopy in pajamas	n/a	$7.00
Linus	n/a	$7.00
Lucy	n/a	$7.00
Woodstock with earmuffs	n/a	$7.00

Colorful Images (Applause)

Charlie Brown	$6.00	$6.00
Snoopy	$6.00	$6.00
Woodstock	$6.00	$6.00

Colorful Images, Holiday 1998 (Applause)

Santa Snoopy	n/a	$6.00
Santa Woodstock	n/a	$6.00

Snoopy & Friends (Irwin Toy)

Snoopy	$5.00	$5.00
Snoopy as Flying Ace	$5.00	$5.00
Snoopy as Joe Cool	$5.00	$5.00
Woodstock	$5.00	$5.00

Raggedy Ann & Andy®

The children's characters Raggedy Ann and Andy have been made into bean bag form by Applause. Raggedy Andy seems to be a little more difficult to find.

Item	S/1999
Raggedy Andy	$6.00
Raggedy Ann	$5.00

Sanrio®

Front: Keroppi (green suit), Keroppi (red suit), Badtz-Maru, Badtz-Maru (pink tear); Back: Hello Kitty (Santa suit), Hello Kitty (pink suit) Hello Kitty (red suit)

"Hello Kitty" is one of several characters from Sanrio. Be sure to check out their neat website at http://www.sanrio.com and find great maps to your local stores carrying their products.

Item	S/1999
Badtz-Maru	$7.00
Badtz-Maru, lying down	$8.00
Badtz-Maru, pink tear	$9.00
Hello Kitty, bumblebee outfit	$9.00
Hello Kitty, bunny suit, pink	$7.00
Hello Kitty, bunny suit, purple	$7.00
Hello Kitty, butterfly outfit	$7.00

Hello Kitty, green suit	$6.00
Hello Kitty, mermaid outfit	$10.00
Hello Kitty, pink suit	$7.00
Hello Kitty, red suit	$7.00
Hello Kitty, Santa suit	$14.00
Hello Kitty, strawberry suit	$9.00
Keroppi, green suit	$6.00
Keroppi, red suit	$6.00
Pochacco, blue suit	$6.00
Pochacco, green suit	$6.00

Scholastic® Bean Bags

Scholastic has featured some children's characters as bean bags.

Item	W/1998	S/1999
Clifford the Big Red Dog	$11.00	$13.00
Liz, The Magic School Bus	$10.00	$10.00

Shamlanders®

This bean bag is a character from the children's book *Shamlanders*.

Item	S/1999
Shamlanders	$10.00

Smokey the Bear®

Remember, only you can prevent forest fires . . . and collect these bean bags. These are very well done, officially-licensed Smokey the Bear bean bags. The holiday Smokey has reportedly been limited to between 6,000 and 10,000.

Smokey the Bear, Christmas limited edition

Item	S/1999
Smokey the Bear	$10.00
Smokey the Bear, Christmas limited edition	$20.00

Toot & Puddle®

Cute characters from the children's book *Toot & Puddle*.

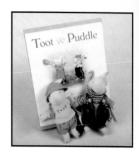

Item	S/1999
Puddle	$7.00
Toot	$7.00

Veggie Friend Seedies & Fruit Seedies®

Front: Skeeter Squash, Belle Pepper, Moy Mushroom; Middle: Beta Carrot, Ripe Tomato, Collie Flower, Cabby Cabbage; Back: Corny the Cob, Spuds Potato, Charles Broccoli, Ollie Onion, Crunchy Celery

Toy Box Creations has developed three lines of fun and educational vegetable and fruit bean bags. They are available in select supermarkets. Check the company's website at http://www.toyboxc.com for great collector information and interesting fruit and veggie trivia (wonderful for kids).

Item	W/1998	S/1999
Fruit Seedies		
Al Avocado	$6.00	$6.00
Ashley Apple	$6.00	$6.00
Golly Grape	$6.00	$7.00
Hula Pineapple	$6.00	$6.00
Luis Lemon	$6.00	$6.00
Peaceful Peach	$6.00	$6.00
Perky Pear	$6.00	$6.00
Slam Banana	$6.00	$6.00
Stu Strawberry	$6.00	$6.00
Sunny Orange	$6.00	$6.00
Tutti Grapefruity	$6.00	$6.00
Wally Watermelon	$6.00	$7.00
Veggie Friend Seedies		
Belle Pepper	$6.00	$6.00
Beta Carrot	$6.00	$6.00
Cabby Cabbage	$6.00	$6.00
Charles Broccoli	$6.00	$7.00
Collie Flower	$6.00	$6.00
Corny on the Cob	$6.00	$6.00
Crunchy Celery	$6.00	$6.00
Moy Mushroom	$8.00	$7.00
Ollie Onion	$7.00	$6.00

Ripe Tomato	$6.00	$6.00
Skeeter Squash	$6.00	$6.00
Spuds Potato	$6.00	$6.00

Veggie Friend Seedies from Around the World

Ima Farmer Corn	$7.00	$8.00
Izzy Zucchini	$7.00	$7.00
Ming Mushroom	$7.00	$7.00
Mountie Lief Lettuce	$7.00	$7.00
Pepe Pepper	$7.00	$7.00
Pierre Onion	$7.00	$7.00

Winnie-the-Pooh® Bean Bags

Mattel (and its sister company Fisher-Price) has issued several different high-quality bean bags and boxed bean bag sets. These Winnie-the-Pooh bean bags are cute, lovable, and should fare well in the future.

Eeyore, Pooh, Tigger, Piglet

Owl, Rabbit, Gopher, Kanga

Item	W/1998	S/1999
Eeyore	$5.00	$5.00
Gopher	$5.00	$5.00
Kanga	$5.00	$5.00
Owl	$5.00	$5.00
Piglet	$5.00	$5.00
Rabbit	$5.00	$5.00
Tigger	$5.00	$5.00
Winnie-the-Pooh	$5.00	$5.00

Holiday 1998—Eeyore, Pooh, Tigger

Winnie-the-Pooh Beanbag Friends Holiday 1998

Eeyore, Santa hat	n/a	$7.00
Tigger, Santa hat	n/a	$7.00
Winnie-the-Pooh, Santa hat	n/a	$7.00

Small Beanbags—Kanga, Pooh, Tigger, Eeyore, Piglet

Winnie-the-Pooh Small Beanbags

Eeyore, small, Velcro on paws	n/a	$5.00
Kanga, small, Velcro on paws	n/a	$5.00
Piglet, small, Velcro on paws	n/a	$5.00
Piglet, small, Velcro on paws	n/a	$5.00
Tigger, small, Velcro on paws	n/a	$5.00

"Easter Pooh-Rade"   Eeyore, Pooh, Piglet, Tigger
Pooh, Piglet,
Tigger

Winnie-the-Pooh Boxed Sets

"Easter Pooh-Rade" (Pooh, Piglet, Tigger)	n/a	$12.00
"Nature Lovin' Pooh & Friends" (Tigger, Eeyore, Pooh, Piglet)	n/a	$15.00

DiSney
Mini Bean Bag Plush

Disney® Mini Bean Bag Plush

Disney Mini Bean Bag Plush (MBBP) are wonderful, dynamite, and perhaps the most-loved bean bags around. Many are hard to find and very valuable. There are actually more Disney bean bags to collect than Ty Beanie Babies®. It's been difficult for even the best Disney collectors to keep up with the staggering number of new Disney MBBP and the retirements. Thankfully, Disney issued a statement earlier this year that it will decrease the number of monthly releases, restructure the quantity of each character produced in order to enhance later value, and stagger future releases (allowing us determined collectors time to breathe!). Disney has also created a Disney MBBP Hotline for the latest news and character updates. Winnie-the-Pooh is probably the most in-demand character, as there are many Pooh-only collectors outside of bean bag and Disney collectors. Limited edition bean bags, such as those created for specific holidays, are usually the best bet to continue to climb in value.

Disney Address/Phone Book

The Official Disney Mini Bean Bag Plush Website: www.disneymbbp.com

The Disney Beanie Report (the BEST Disney site on the Internet!): http://www.dizbeanies.com

Club Disney, West Covina:	626-938-1499
Club Disney, Thousand Oaks:	805-777-8018
Disney Catalog:	800-237-5751
Disneyland Merchandising:	800-760-3566
Disney MBBP Hotline:	818-265-4280
Walt Disney World Guest Services:	407-363-6200

If you are under eighteen years of age, please be sure to have your parents' permission to utilize these telephone numbers.

Tag Identification

Club Disney
Version 1 (CD1)

Disney Store tag (DST)

Club Disney
Version 2 (CD2)

Walt Disney
World tag
(WDW)

Mouseketoys tag (MKT)

In the United States you can find several tag variations. The most common hang-tag on Disney Mini Bean Bags is the Disney Store hang-tag. The Club Disney hang-tag was changed from small to large during 1998.

The International hang-tag can be found on Disney Bean Bags from countries other than the United States, with the exception of Japan and Paris, who each have their own type of hang-tag. The Japan tag's only difference is on the back, with the price in yen.

A number of "extra" hang-tags have been created for the Disney Mini Bean Bags. These are special tags created for special sets of bean bags or special events. Often, movie-character bean bags will have the additional movie hang-tag on them now. For instance, the red "Mulan" tag is on the bean bag characters from the movie *Mulan*.

15th Anniversary
Disneyland Japan

Animal Kingdom

Classic Pooh

International hang-tags (INTL)

it's a small world

Monochrome Set

Club Disney
Signed Merlin

Mickey Mouse 70th
Anniversary

Disney Lingo
DL: Disneyland
DS: Disney Store
LE: Limited edition characters that are themed to a season or holiday for a specific year. A limited quantity is produced.
MBBP: Mini Bean Bag Plush
(R): Retired characters are no longer in production. Some may still be available, but only while supplies last.
Sound: Bean bag with mechanism to make noise or give it a voice.
Test: One of the "test market" bean bags offered by Disney; the "test" version of the bean bag.
TTNT: Tiny Tush Name Tag
V1, V2, etc.: Version 1, Version 2, etc.
WDW: Walt Disney World

101 Dalmatians

Lucky, Patch, Penny

Top: Cruella De Vil, Jewel; Middle: 101 Pup V1, 101 Pup V2, 101 Pup V3, Lucky V2; Bottom: Lucky V3, Lucky V1

Item	W/1998	S/1999
101 Dalmatians Pup (Test: "V" on forehead, no spots on belly) (R)	$55.00	$30.00
101 Dalmatians Pup (V2: no "V" on forehead, spots on belly) (R)	$20.00	$14.00
101 Dalmatians Pup (V3: "V" on forehead, spots on belly) (R)	$14.00	$12.00
Cruella De Vil (R)	$7.00	$8.00
Jewel (R)	$12.00	$10.00
Lucky (French, red collar)	$24.00	$15.00
Lucky (V1: no "V" on forehead, larger head, $9 or $10 sticker) (R)	$22.00	$14.00
Lucky (V2: "V" on forehead) (R)	$30.00	$16.00
Lucky (V3: no "V" on forehead, smaller head, no $9 sticker) (R)	$8.00	$8.00
Lucky (Sound) n/a $8.00		
Patch (French, green collar)	$30.00	$16.00
Penny (French, pink collar)	$28.00	$16.00
Penny (Sound)	n/a	$8.00

Abominable Snowman

Item	S/1999
Abominable Snowman (DL Exclusive)	$12.00

Aladdin

Item	W/1998	S/1999
Abu	$7.00	$7.00
Aladdin (R)	$7.00	$8.00
Genie	$7.00	$7.00
Iago	$7.00	$7.00
Jafar	$7.00	$7.00
Jasmine (R)	$8.00	$8.00

Abu, Aladdin, Genie, Jafar, Iago

Alice in Wonderland

Top: Alice, Queen of Hearts, Cheshire Cat; Bottom: March Hare, White Rabbit, Mad Hatter, Red Card, Black Card, Tweedle Dee, Tweedle Dum

Item	W/1998	S/1999
Alice	n/a	$7.00
Black Card	$30.00	$7.00
Cheshire Cat	$60.00	$8.00
Mad Hatter	$30.00	$7.00
March Hare	n/a	$7.00
Queen of Hearts	$32.00	$7.00
Red Card	$30.00	$8.00
Tweedle Dee (discontinued)	$24.00	$15.00
Tweedle Dum (discontinued)	$24.00	$15.00
Tweedle Dee/Tweedle Dum (attached)	n/a	$14.00
White Rabbit	$23.00	$7.00

Animal Kingdom

Top:
Brontosaurus,
Triceratops, T-Rex;
Middle: Spider;
Bottom: Tree Frog,
Red Ant

Item	W/1998	S/1999
Bee	n/a	$7.00
Brontosaurus	$15.00	$9.00
Red Ant	n/a	$12.00
Spider (yellow and black)	n/a	$9.00
Tree Frog (V1: MKT Tags)	$500.00	$225.00
Tree Frog (V2: WDW Tags)	$25.00	$15.00
T-Rex	$15.00	$9.00
Triceratops	$15.00	$9.00

Aristocats

Duchess V1, Duchess V2, Marie V1, Marie V2

Item	W/1998	S/1999
Duchess (V1: with whiskers)	$18.00	$18.00
Duchess (V2: without whiskers)	$7.00	$7.00
Marie (V1: 7", lighter pink bows)	$15.00	$9.00
Marie (V2: 8", darker pink bows)	$7.00	$7.00

Bambi

Bambi, Flower, Thumper V1, Thumper V2

Item	W/1998	S/1999
Bambi (R)	$10.00	$8.00
Flower (R)	$10.00	$8.00
Thumper (Chocolate Egg, LE 1999)	n/a	$22.00
Thumper (V1: plain chest) (R)	$10.00	$8.00
Thumper (V2: fuzzy chest) (R)	$14.00	$8.00

Beauty and the Beast

Top: Belle, Beast;
Bottom: Cogsworth, Mrs.
Potts, Chip, Lumier

Cogsworth, Lumiere

Item	S/1999
The Beast	$7.00
Belle	$7.00
Chip	$7.00
Cogsworth	$7.00
Cogsworth (Broadway Show, bigger)	$12.00*
Lumiere	$7.00
Lumiere (Broadway Show, bigger)	$12.00*
Mrs. Potts	$7.00

*These were only available for purchase at the
Broadway Show production of *Beauty and the Beast*.

Black Cauldron

Item	W/1998	S/1999
Fairfolk (R)	$8.00	$8.00
Gurgi (R)	$8.00	$8.00
Hen Wen (R)	$8.00	$8.00

A Bug's Life

Item	S/1999
Atta (R)	$7.00
Dim (R)	$7.00
Dot (R)	$7.00
Flik (R)	$7.00
Francis (R)	$7.00
Heimlich (R)	$7.00
Heimlich (Sound)	$8.00
Hopper	$7.00
P.T. Flea (R)	$7.00
Roll	$7.00
Rosie Spider	$7.00
Tuck	$7.00

Top: Flik, Heimlich, Hopper; Bottom: Dim, Francis, Dot, Atta

Chip and Dale

Chip V1, Chip V2, Dale V1, Dale V2

Item	W/1998	S/1999
Chip (V1: brown) (R)	$7.00	$7.00
Chip (V2: reddish-brown) (R)	$8.00	$8.00
Chip (V3: furry, Japan exclusive)	n/a	$15.00
Dale (V1: brown) (R)	$7.00	$7.00
Dale (V2: reddish-brown) (R)	$8.00	$8.00
Dale (V3: furry, Japan exclusive)	n/a	$15.00

Cinderella

Item	W/1998	S/1999
Gus (R)	$7.00	$8.00
Jaq (R)	$7.00	$8.00
Suzy (R)	$7.00	$8.00

Gus, Jaq, Suzy

Disneyland Paris Halloween Trio

Item	S/1999
Devil	$14.00
Pumpkin	$14.00
Witch	$14.00

Devil, Pumpkin, Witch

Doug

Item	S/1999
Doug	$7.00
Patti	$7.00
Porkchop	$7.00

Doug, Patti, Porkchop

Dumbo

Top: Dumbo V1, Dumbo V2, Dumbo V3, Dumbo V4;
Bottom: Timothy V1, Timothy V2, Timothy V3

Item	W/1998	S/1999
Dumbo (V1: blue ruffle, no feather, no foam in ears)	$10.00	$8.00
Dumbo (V2: blue ruffle, feather, no foam in ears)	$12.00	$8.00
Dumbo (V3: yellow ruffle, feather, no foam in ears)	$10.00	$12.00
Dumbo (V4: blue ruffle, no feather, foam in ears)	$7.00	$7.00
Timothy (V1: standing)	$7.00	$7.00
Timothy (V2: sitting)	$12.00	$12.00
Timothy (V3: sitting, WDCC tag*)	$75.00	$25.00

* This special tag was created for Timothy V3, which came with an ornament. The abbreviation stands for "Walt Disney Classics Collection."

Fantasia

Item	W/1998	S/1999
Ben Ali Gator	$8.00	$8.00
Hyacinth the Hippo	$8.00	$8.00
Sorcerer Mickey	$10.00	$8.00

Ben Ali Gator, Hyacinth,
Sorcerer Mickey

Figment

Item	W/1998	S/1999
Figment (R)	$22.00	$15.00
Figment (Disney Cruise, with certificate and life preserver)	n/a	$450.00

Flubber

Item	W/1998	S/1999
Flubber (R)	$35.00	$28.00
Flubber (Sound) (R)	$18.00	$10.00

Flubber

George of the Jungle

Shep, George, Ape

Item	S/1999
Ape (R)	$8.00
George (R)	$8.00
Shep (R)	$8.00

Herbie, The Love Bug

item	W/1998	S/1999
Herbie (R)	$ 9.00	$10.00

Hercules

Baby Pegasus, Pain, Panic

Item	W/1998	S/1999
Baby Pegasus (R)	$35.00	$35.00
Pain (LE 1997)	$9.00	$8.00
Panic (LE 1997)	$9.00	$8.00

it's a small world

Item	S/1999
Africa Boy	$9.00
Alaska Boy	$7.00
Belgium Girl	$8.00
China Girl	$7.00
England Boy	$7.00
French Girl	$15.00
Hawaii Girl	n/a
Holland Girl	$7.00
India Girl	$15.00
Japan Girl	$7.00
Mexico Boy	$7.00
Mexico Girl	$12.00
Middle East Girl	$10.00
Native American Indian Boy	$12.00

Top: England Boy, Holland Girl, Alaska Boy; Bottom: Mexico Boy, Japan Girl, China Girl

Pink and Purple Striped Zebra, DL exclusive (R)	$12.00	
Pink/Flowered Hippo, DL exclusive (R)	$12.00	
Pink/Flowered Kangaroo and Joey, DL exclusive (R)	$12.00	
Pink/Flowered Rhino, DL exclusive (R)	$12.00	
Russia Girl	n/a	
Russia Boy	n/a	
Sweden Girl	n/a	

Jungle Book

Item	W/1998	S/1999
Bagheera	$10.00	$8.00
Baloo	$9.00	$7.00
King Louie	$10.00	$7.00

Bagheera, Baloo, King Louie

Lady and the Tramp

Trusty, Lady, Tramp V1, Tramp V2, Jock

Lady 2

Item	W/1998	S/1999
Jock	$7.00	$7.00
Lady (V1: red collar)	$7.00	$7.00
Lady (V2: blue collar, UK Exclusive with video purchase)	n/a	$22.00
Tramp (V1)	$7.00	$7.00
Tramp (V2: reddish-brown collar, slightly smaller)	$7.00	$7.00
Trusty	$7.00	$7.00

Lion King

Top: Banzai, Ed, Shenzi;
Bottom: Scar, Timon,
Pumbaa, Simba, Nala,
Rafiki, Zazu

Item	W/1998	S/1999
Banzai	n/a	$7.00
Ed	n/a	$7.00
Nala	$14.00	$7.00
Pumbaa	$7.00	$7.00
Pumbaa (Sound)	n/a	$8.00
Rafiki	$8.00	$7.00
Scar	n/a	$7.00
Shenzi	n/a	$7.00
Simba	$13.00	$7.00
Timon	$7.00	$7.00
Zazu	$7.00	$7.00

Lion King II: Simba's Pride

Item	W/1998	S/1999
Kiara	$8.00	$7.00
Kovu	$8.00	$7.00

Kiara, Kovu

Lion King Broadway Musical

Item	S/1999
Nala	$10.00
Pumbaa	$10.00
Simba	$10.00
Timon	$10.00
Trickster #1	$10.00
Trickster #2	$10.00
Trickster #3	$10.00
Trickster #4	$10.00
Trickster #5	$10.00
Zazu	$10.00

Tricksters

Little Mermaid

Top: Ariel, Eric, Ursula; Bottom: Flounder—Test, V2, V3;
Sebastian—Test, V2, V3

Item	W/1998	S/1999
Ariel (R)	$8.00	$8.00
Eric (R)	$8.00	$8.00
Flounder (Test: shorter, feelers, all seams, "CDN $10" on tag) (R)	$25.00	$12.00
Flounder (V2: longer, bigger mouth, feelers, all seams) (R)	$15.00	$9.00
Flounder (V3: all one piece to fin, no seams on any fins) (R)	$15.00	$10.00
Sebastian (Test: seam on back, segmented claws) (R)	$25.00	$12.00
Sebastian (V2: no seam on back, segmented claws) (R)	$15.00	$10.00
Sebastian (V3: no seam on back, not segmented claws) (R)	$16.00	$10.00
Ursula	$10.00	$8.00

Mary Poppins

Item	S/1999
Bert	$7.00
Fox	$7.00
Mary	$7.00
Penguin	$7.00

Top: Fox, Penguin;
Bottom: Mary Poppins,
Bert

Merlin

Item	W/1998	S/1999
Merlin (Club Disney exclusive)	$15.00	$10.00
Merlin, signed (stamped tag)*	$80.00	$35.00

*See tag identification section at
beginning of Disney MBBP section

Mickey and Friends

Daisy V1, Daisy V2

Item	W/1998	S/1999
Daisy (V1: sewn eyes) (R)	$7.00	$9.00
Daisy (V2: plastic eyes, more plush) (R)	$8.00	$10.00
Daisy (Tomorrowland) (R)	n/a	$10.00

Donald Duck—Top: Soccer, Tomorrowland, Monochrome;
Bottom: Test, V2, V3

Item	W/1998	S/1999
Donald (Test: sewn tuck on hat, flag in front of hat)	$18.00	$15.00
Donald (V2: untucked hat, flag in back)	$7.00	$7.00
Donald (V3: plastic eyes, more plush)	$8.00	$8.00
Donald (Monochrome)	$45.00	$25.00
Donald (Soccer, LE 1998)	$175.00	$115.00
Donald (Tomorrowland) (R)	$8.00	$8.00
Donald (65th Anniversary set of 4)	n/a	$36.00

Goofy—Top: Test, V2, V3;
Bottom: Tomorrowland

Item	W/1998	S/1999
Goofy (Test: beans in arms and legs) (R)	$20.00	$18.00
Goofy (V2: beans not in legs) (R)	$7.00	$7.00
Goofy (V3: plastic eyes, more plush) (R)	$8.00	$8.00
Goofy (Cowboy)	n/a	n/a
Goofy (Gradnite, LE 1999)	n/a	n/a
Goofy (Tomorrowland) (R)	$8.00	$8.00
Goofy (Uncle Sam)	n/a	$8.00

Item	W/1998	S/1999
Huey/Dewey/Louie (V1: mistake colors-blue/green/red, smaller, hat sideways) (R)	$45.00	$36.00

Huey/Dewey/Louie—Front: V1; Back: V3

Huey/Dewey/Louie—Front: V2; Back: V4

Huey/Dewey/Louie (V2: mistake colors-blue/green/red, larger, more plush, hat forward) (R)	$40.00	$32.00
Huey/Dewey/Louie (V3: correct colors-red/blue/green, smaller, hat sideways) (R)	$24.00	$24.00
Huey/Dewey/Louie (V4: correct colors-red/blue/green, larger, more plush, hat forward) (R)	$24.00	$22.00
Huey/Dewey/Louie (Frontierland)	n/a	$30.00

Mickey, 70th Anniversary Set

	W/1998	S/1999
Mickey (Test: 9", no black stitching around eyes and mouth) (R)	$80.00	$45.00
Mickey (V2: 8", less stuffing, more beans) (R)	$15.00	$12.00
Mickey (V3: smaller, completely beans) (R)	$9.00	$8.00
Mickey (V4: plastic eyes, more plush) (R)	$10.00	$9.00
Mickey (70th Anniversary Set, in hat, pants) (R)	$35.00	$35.00
Mickey (1930s-style)	$18.00	$25.00
Mickey (Adventure, DL Paris Exclusive)	n/a	$15.00
Mickey (Cast Member, LE 1997)	$425.00	$300.00

Mickey—Top: Test, V2, V3, V4; Bottom: Gradnite WDW, Disney Quest, Chinese New Year, 1930s-style, Gradnite DL

Mickey—Top: Jester V1, Monochrome, Soccer; Bottom: Valentine, Santa, Nutcracker

Mickey—Top: Tomorrowland, Scarecrow, Spirit of Mickey; Bottom: Tourist, Toga, Pilot

Mickey (Chinese New Year V1: all white gloves, Hong Kong)	$90.00	$75.00
Mickey (Chinese New Year V2: black lines on gloves, Hong Kong)	n/a	$20.00
Mickey (Club Disney)	$9.00	$9.00
Mickey (Discoveryland, DL Paris Exclusive)	n/a	$22.00
Mickey (Disney Quest)	n/a	$11.00
Mickey (Fantasyland, DL Paris Exclusive)	n/a	$24.00
Mickey (Frontierland, DL Paris Exclusive)	n/a	$20.00
Mickey (Gradnite, DL, LE 1998)	$30.00	$22.00
Mickey (Gradnite, WDW, floral shorts, LE 1998)	$40.00	$25.00
Mickey (Jester V1) (R)	$50.00	$35.00
Mickey (Jester V2: Christmas)	n/a	$46.00
Mickey (Kimono)	n/a	$30.00
Mickey (Mainstreet, DL Paris Exclusive)	n/a	$26.00
Mickey (Monochrome)	$44.00	$25.00
Mickey (Nutcracker, LE 1998)	n/a	$8.00
Mickey (Palace Guard, UK Exclusive)	n/a	$25.00
Mickey (Pilot)	$9.00	$7.00
Mickey (Santa, LE 1997)	$9.00	$9.00
Mickey (Scarecrow, LE 1998)	$12.00	$11.00
Mickey (Soccer, LE 1998)	$150.00	$100.00
Mickey (Spirit of Mickey, LE 1998)	$10.00	$14.00
Mickey (Toga)	$7.00	$7.00
Mickey (Tomorrowland) (R)	$8.00	$8.00
Mickey (Tourist)	$7.00	$7.00
Mickey (Valentine, LE 1998)	$20.00	$17.00

Mickey—Top: Mainstreet, Discoveryland, Fantasyland; Bottom: Frontierland, Adventure

	W/1998	S/1999

Minnie—Top: Test, V2, V3, V4; Bottom: 1930s-style, Chinese New Year, Disney Quest, Hula

Minnie (Test: 9", no black around eyes and mouth) (R)
| | $80.00 | $45.00 |

Minnie (V2: 8", less dots on dress) (R)
| | $10.00 | $10.00 |

Minnie (V3: 7", more dots on dress) (R)
| | $9.00 | $9.00 |

Minnie (V4: plastic eyes, more plush) (R)
| | $9.00 | $9.00 |

Minnie (1930s-style)
| | $18.00 | $25.00 |

Minnie (Chinese New Year V1: all white gloves, Hong Kong)
| | $90.00 | $75.00 |

Minnie (Chinese New Year V2: black lines on gloves, Hong Kong)
| | n/a | $20.00 |

Minnie (Club Disney)
| | $9.00 | $9.00 |

Minnie (Disney Quest)
| | n/a | $11.00 |

Minnie (Hula)
| | $10.00 | $8.00 |

Minnie (Jester V1) (R)
| | $50.00 | $35.00 |

Minnie (Jester V2: Christmas)
| | n/a | $46.00 |

Minnie—Top: Jester V1, Monochrome, Liberty; Bottom: Sugar Plum, Tomorrowland, Spirit of Mickey, Santa, Valentine

	W/1998	S/1999
Minnie (Kimono)	n/a	$30.00
Minnie (Liberty)	$9.00	$8.00
Minnie (Monochrome)	$45.00	$25.00
Minnie (Princess)	n/a	$7.00
Minnie (Santa, LE 1997)	$9.00	$9.00
Minnie (Spirit of Mickey, LE 1998)	$10.00	$14.00
Minnie (Sugar Plum Fairy, LE 1998)	n/a	$12.00
Minnie (Tomorrowland) (R)	$8.00	$8.00
Minnie (Valentine, LE 1998)	$20.00	$17.00

Pluto—Top: Test, V2, V3; Bottom: Reindeer, Tomorrowland

Pluto (Test: tag says 9", longer ears, footpads on hind feet) (R)
| | $20.00 | $24.00 |

Pluto (V2: tag has no measurement, no footpads) (R)
| | $7.00 | $7.00 |

Pluto (V3: plastic eyes, more plush) (R)
| | $8.00 | $8.00 |

Pluto (Reindeer, LE 1997)
| | $24.00 | $21.00 |

Pluto (Tomorrowland) (R)
| | $8.00 | $8.00 |

Mighty Joe Young

Item	S/1999
Mighty Joe Young (R)	$12.00

Mulan

Item	W/1998	S/1999
Cri-Kee (R)	$8.00	$9.00
Khan	n/a	$7.00
Lil' Brother (R)	$7.00	$7.00
Lil' Brother (Sound)	n/a	$8.00
Mulan (Traditional)	n/a	$7.00
Mulan (Warrior)	n/a	$7.00
Mu-Shu	$10.00	$7.00
Mu-Shu (Sound) (R)	$10.00	$9.00

Top: Cri-Kee, Mulan (Warrior), Mulan (Traditional); Bottom: Khan, Mu-Shu, Lil' Brother

Oliver & Co.

Item	S/1999
Dodger	$7.00
Oliver	$7.00

Oliver, Dodger

The Parent Trap

Item	S/1999
Cuppy Bunny	$10.00

Peter Pan

Captain Hook, Crock, Nana, Peter Pan, Smee

Item	W/1998	S/1999
Captain Hook (R)	$9.00	$8.00
Crock (R)	$8.00	$8.00
Nana (R)	$9.00	$8.00
Peter Pan (R)	$8.00	$8.00
Smee (R)	$9.00	$8.00

Pinocchio

Figaro, Geppetto, Jiminy Cricket, Pinocchio

Item	W/1998	S/1999
Figaro (R)	$10.00	$8.00
Geppetto (R)	$9.00	$8.00
Jiminy Cricket	$9.00	$8.00
Pinocchio (R)	$9.00	$8.00

Rescuers

Item	S/1999
Bernard	$7.00
Bianca	$7.00
Orville	$7.00

Bianca, Orville, Bernard

Robin Hood

Lady Kluck, Maid Marian, Robin Hood, Prince John, Little Joh[n]

Item	W/1998	S/1999
Lady Kluck (R)	$7.00	$7.00
Little John (R)	$7.00	$7.00
Maid Marian (R)	$7.00	$7.00
Prince John (R)	$7.00	$7.00
Robin Hood (R)	$7.00	$7.00

Sleeping Beauty

Item	W/1998	S/1999
Maleficent	$8.00	$7.00
Maleficent (Dragon)	$8.00	$7.00
Prince Phillip (R)	n/a	$7.00
Princess Aurora (R)	$8.00	$7.00

Top: Prince Phillip, Princess Aurora;
Bottom: Maleficent Dragon, Maleficent

Snow White and the Seven Dwarfs

Item	W/1998	S/1999
Bashful (R)	$20.00	$12.00
Doc (R)	$10.00	$12.00
Dopey (Test: "Beanbag" all one word on tag) (R)	$40.00	$25.00
Dopey (V2: "Bean Bag" two words on tag) (R)	$14.00	$10.00
Hag	$7.00	$7.00
Grumpy (Test: "Beanbag" all one word on tag) (R)	$42.00	$20.00
Grumpy (V2: "Bean Bag" two		

Snow White, Prince, Hag

Top: Dopey, Doc; Bottom:
Bashful, Grumpy, Happy,
Sleepy, Sneezy

words on tag) (R)
$10.00	$9.00
Happy (R)	
$16.00	$12.00
Prince from Snow White (R)	
$7.00	$7.00
Sleepy (R)	
$13.00	$12.00
Sneezy (R)	
$12.00	$10.00
Snow White (R)	
$7.00	$7.00

Song of the South

Bear, Fox, Rabbit, Vulture

Item	W/1998	S/1999
Brer Bear	$9.00	$8.00
Brer Fox	$9.00	$8.00
Brer Rabbit	$9.00	$8.00
Vulture	$9.00	$8.00

Toy Story

Top: Woody V1, Woody
V2, Rex; Bottom: Buzz
V1, Buzz V2, Alien,
Hamm

Item	W/1998	S/1999
Alien	$7.00	$7.00
Buzz Lightyear		
(V1: "V" on chest, kneepads)		
	$12.00	$10.00
Buzz Lightyear		
(V2: no "V," no kneepads)		
	$7.00	$7.00
Hamm	$7.00	$7.00
Hamm (JPN Tag)		
	$16.00	$12.00
Rex	$7.00	$7.00
Woody		
(V1: buttons on shirt, cuffs, lines on hat)		
	$10.00	$9.00
Woody (V2: no buttons on shirt, no cuffs, no lines on hat)		
	$7.00	$7.00

Winnie-the-Pooh and Friends

Top: Gopher, Gopher-Bunny, Owl V1, Kanga V1; Bottom: Rabbit V1, Rabbit V2, Christopher Robin, Owl V2, Roo, Kanga V2

Item	W/1998	S/1999
Christopher Robin (R)	$8.00	$7.00

Eeyore—Top: Test, V2, V3, V4; Bottom: Reindeer V1, Reindeer V2, Cupid, Sugar Plum, Classic

Eeyore (Test: smaller, shorter nose, more plush)	$15.00	$15.00
Eeyore (V2: longer, longer nose)	$7.00	$7.00
Eeyore (V3: much darker)	$8.00	$8.00
Eeyore (V4: gray)	$14.00	$12.00
Eeyore (Classic)	$7.00	$7.00
Eeyore (Cupid)	n/a	$11.00
Eeyore (Dinosaur, LE 1998)	$12.00	$13.00
Eeyore (Reindeer V1: lighter blue, smaller bow, LE 1997)	$14.00	$15.00
Eeyore (Reindeer V2: darker blue, bigger bow, LE 1997)	$14.00	$15.00

Eeyore (Sugar Plum Fairy)		
(LE 1998)	n/a	$14.00
Gopher (R)	$9.00	$8.00
Gopher (Bunny)	n/a	$12.00
Heffalump #4 (blue/pink/yellow)	n/a	$8.00

Kanga (V1: 8")		
$8.00	$8.00	
Kanga (V2: 7")		
$7.00	$7.00	
Owl (V1: plain chin)		
$7.00	$7.00	
Owl (V2: fuzzy chin)		
$9.00	$8.00	

Heffalump #4
(blue/pink/yellow)

Piglet (Test: footpads)		
$35.00	$28.00	
Piglet (V2: no footpads)		
$7.00	$7.00	
Piglet (Classic)		
$8.00	$7.00	
Piglet (Easter Egg, LE 1999)		
n/a	$8.00	
Piglet (Pumpkin, UK		
Exclusive, LE 1998)		
n/a	$85.00	
Piglet (Valentine, UK		
Exclusive, LE 1999)		
n/a	$22.00	

Piglet—Top: Pumpkin,
Valentine, Easter Egg;
Bottom: Test, V2, Classic

Rabbit (V1: yellow tail)	$7.00	$7.00
Rabbit (V2: white tail)	$8.00	$8.00
Roo	n/a	$7.00

Tigger—Top: V2, V4;
Bottom: Test, V3, V5

Tigger—Top: Mad Scientist,
St. Patrick's Day; Bottom:
Classic V2, Classic V1,
Xmas V1, Xmas V2

Tigger (Test: footpads, straight		
tail, fewer stripes)	$55.00	$32.00

Tigger (V2: no footpads, curly tail, fewer stripes)	$28.00	$20.00
Tigger (V3: no footpads, curly tail, more stripes)	$8.00	$8.00
Tigger (V4: no footpads, straight tail, more stripes)	$10.00	$10.00
Tigger (V5: footpads, curly tail, bigger eyebrows)	$7.00	$7.00
Tigger (Classic V1: orange) (R)	$8.00	$7.00
Tigger (Classic V2: brownish-orange) (R)	$8.00	$7.00
Tigger (Gradnite, LE 1999)	n/a	n/a
Tigger (Mad Scientist, LE 1998)	$10.00	$15.00
Tigger (St. Patrick's Day, LE 1999)	n/a	$24.00
Tigger (Xmas V1: small eyebrows, no footpads, LE 1997)	$30.00	$25.00
Tigger (Xmas V2: bigger eyebrows, footpads, UK Exclusive, LE 1998)	n/a	$32.00

Pooh—Test, V2, V3, Choo-Choo, Classic

Winnie-the-Pooh (Test: footpads, hard nose)	$33.00	$32.00
Winnie-the-Pooh (V2: no footpads, hard nose)	$10.00	$12.00
Winnie-the-Pooh (V3: no footpads, stitched nose)	$7.00	$7.00
Winnie the Pooh (Baseball)	n/a	$8.00
Winnie-the-Pooh (Bumblebee)	$9.00	$8.00
Winnie-the-Pooh (Choo-Choo) (R)	n/a	$9.00
Winnie-the-Pooh (Classic) (R)	$8.00	$7.00
Winnie-the-Pooh (Easter, lavender bunny suit, DST only, LE 1998)	$85.00	$70.00
Winnie-the-Pooh (Easter, red shirt, bunny ears, LE 1998)	$42.00	$35.00
Winnie-the-Pooh (Easter Bunny, blue, LE 1999)	n/a	$14.00
Winnie-the-Pooh (Easter Bunny, white, LE 1999, Japan Exclusive)	n/a	$25.00
Winnie-the-Pooh (Gradnite, DL, LE 1998)	$30.00	$24.00
Winnie-the-Pooh (Gradnite, WDW, floral shorts, LE 1998)	$36.00	$28.00
Winnie-the-Pooh (Hanukkah, LE 1998)	n/a	$12.00

Winnie-the-Pooh (Pilot) (R)	$8.00	$9.00
Winnie-the-Pooh (Pumpkin) (LE 1998)	$12.00	$12.00
Winnie-the-Pooh (Santa V1: hard nose, LE 1997)	$12.00	$24.00

Pooh—Easter (lavender suit), Easter (red shirt), Easter Bunny, Gradnite DL, Gradnite WDW

Winnie-the-Pooh (Santa, V2: stitched nose, LE 1997)	$18.00	$18.00
Winnie-the-Pooh (Snowflake, LE 1998)	n/a	$52.00
Winnie-the-Pooh (Snowman, LE 1998)	n/a	$13.00

Pooh—Top: Hanukkah, Santa V1, Santa V2, Xmas, Snowman; Bottom: Pumpkin, Red Sweater, Snowflake, Pilot, Valentine, Bumblebee

Winnie-the-Pooh (Valentine, LE 1998)	$100.00	$82.00
Winnie-the-Pooh (w/red sweater, LE 1999)	n/a	$12.00
Winnie-the-Pooh (Xmas, green scarf, LE 1997)	$24.00	$30.00
Woozle #2 (pink/fuscia)	n/a	$7.00
Woozle #3 (yellow/green)	n/a	$7.00

Miscellaneous Individuals & Groups

Carlton Cards® Graduation Dog

Produced for Carlton Cards stores in 1997.

Item	W/1998	S/1999
Carlton Cards Graduation Dog (R)	$6.00	$5.00

Hallmark®

Hallmark has sold several Hallmark-only bean bags.

Baby Nikki, Floyd, Little Bounder

Item	W/1998	S/1999
Baby Nikki (R)	$7.00	$8.00
Little Bounder	n/a	$6.00
Floyd (Maxine's sidekick)	n/a	$5.00

Ho Ho Beans®

Santa, Bear

Sold exclusively at Sears during the holiday season.

Item	S/1999
Bear, brown with Santa hat	$6.00
Santa	$6.00

Mystery "Caramel Apple" Bean Bag

I ran across this odd-looking bean bag and bought it. I think it might be a caramel apple, but I'm not sure. If you know something about it, please write to me!

Item	S/1999
Mystery "caramel apple?" bean bag	$8.00

Your guess is as good as mine!

Rainforest Café®

This Christmas tree frog bean bag was sold at the Rainforest Café over the 1998 holiday season.

Item	S/1999
Cha! Cha! Tree frog with Santa hat	$10.00

Tesco®

Offered in the UK, these bean bags are hard to find in our neck of the woods.

Item	S/1999
Chilly the snowman	$10.00
Squeaky Penguin	$10.00

Chilly the snowman, Squeaky Penguin

White's® Santa and Mrs. Claus Bean Bag Dolls

White's Guide to Collecting Figures-issued bean bags. Still available for sale from White's at time of printing.

Santa, Mrs. Claus

Item	W/1998	S/1999
Mrs. Claus, White's Guide Exclusive #27	$8.00	$8.00
Santa, White's Guide Exclusive #26	$8.00	$8.00

MoVie, Tv, &Music Themed

A&A Plush®

A&A Plush made the famous cartoon crow tandem of Heckle & Jeckle into bean bags. They attach at their arms by Velcro.

Mighty Mouse, Heckle & Jeckle

Item	S/1999
Heckle & Jeckle	$12.00
Mighty Mouse	$14.00

An All Dog's Christmas®

Denny's 1998 holiday promotion. Excellent quality.

Item	S/1999
Itchy	$5.00
Scratchy	$5.00

Alvin and the Chipmunks®

Nice Gund-made set of these helium-voiced cartoon characters.

Item	S/1999
Alvin	$7.00
Simon	$7.00
Theodore	$7.00

Alvin, Simon, Theodore

Babar®

Children's storybook/animated film characters were offered in bean bag form in 1997. Made by Gund.

Item	S/1999
Babar the elephant	$10.00
Celeste the elephant	$12.00

Babe®

Gund's Babe was sold at stores and offered as a premium in 1998 (through an offer from Dole); either way, the Babe is the same. The bean bags were released in 1997.

Babe

Item	S/1999
Equity Toys	
Babe: Pig in the City	$6.00
Gund	
Babe the pig	$8.00
Ferdinand the goose	$8.00
Fly the dog	$8.00
Maa the sheep	$8.00

Baby Looney Tunes Bean Toons® (Play-By-Play)

Made by Play-By-Play. Baby Lola Bunny and Baby Wile E. seem to be difficult to find.

Item	S/1999
Baby Bugs	$4.00
Baby Lola Bunny	n/a
Baby Sylvester	$4.00
Baby Taz	$4.00
Baby Tweety	$4.00
Baby Wile E.	n/a

Tweety, Sylvester, Taz, Bugs

Barney®

Gund bean bags of this popular PBS children's show character have been available for a couple of years.

Item	S/1999
Baby Bop	$5.00
Barney	$5.00

Barney, Baby Bop

Bear in the Big Blue House®

From the Disney Channel and the Jim Henson Company, *Bear in the Big Blue House* is a great children's show. This Fisher-Price set offers perfect renditions of the characters. This set was purchased at a Target store.

Item	S/1999
Bear	$7.00
Ojo	$7.00
Treelo	$7.00
Tutter	$7.00

Bear, Tutter, Ojo, Treelo

Big Comfy Couch®

A set of two bean bags was issued for this PBS children's show. These were sold singly or in a boxed set.

Item	S/1999
Loonette	$9.00
Mollie	$7.00

Molly, Loonette,

Blue's Clues®

This Nickelodeon program is entertaining for children (and for the adults who watch it with their children). The bean bags are popular sellers. Expect more characters to be made into bean bags.

Back: Blue, Magenta; Front: Mott's Blue

Item	S/1999
Blockbuster Video Blue	$10.00
Blockbuster Video Magenta	$11.00
Mott's Blue (with birthday hat)	$9.00

A Bug's Life® (Mattel)

Pair of boxed sets made to include characters from this hit Disney animated film.

Bug Bunch, Bug Circus

Item	S/1999
Bug Circus, boxed set of 5 characters, including 2 bean bags (Heimlich, Francis)	$15.00
Bug Bunch, boxed set of 3 (Flik, Princess Dot, Atta)	$12.00

Cartoon Network®

This small Cartoon Network set was available at Target, but has since been hard to find. They may be retired. The four-bean bag Scooby-Doo set was out in K-mart stores about February 1999, and was attached to Scooby-Doo shirts. This set might be in high demand in the future.

Scooby, Tom, Huckleberry Hound, Yogi, Droopy, Jerry

Item	W/1998	S/1999
Target set		
Droopy	$10.00	$7.00
Huckleberry Hound	$8.00	$7.00
Jerry the mouse	$8.00	$10.00
Scooby-Doo	$10.00	$12.00
Tom the cat	$8.00	$10.00
Yogi Bear	$9.00	$10.00

K-mart Scooby-Doos

K-mart Scooby-Doo set		
Scooby, sitting, pink tie-dye shirt	n/a	$8.00
Scooby, sitting, purple tie-dye shirt	n/a	$8.00
Scooby, standing, flowered shorts	n/a	$8.00
Scooby, standing, tie-dye shorts	n/a	$8.00

CVS: Misfits®

In 1998, the East Coast-based CVS Pharmacy issued bean bag versions of the "Isle of Misfit Toys" characters from the Christmas classic *Rudolph the Red-Nosed Reindeer*. This fantastic set is made by Stuffins.

Misfit Train, King Moonracer, Spotted Elephant, Herbie, Charlie in the Box, Misfit Doll

Item	S/1999
Abominable Snowman	$14.00
Charlie in the Box	$10.00
Clarice	$12.00
Herbie	$9.00
Misfit Doll	$7.00
Misfit Train	$7.00
King Moonracer	$7.00
Rudolph	$12.00
Sam the Snowman	$11.00
Santa Claus	$9.00
Spotted Elephant	$9.00
Yukon Cornelius	$10.00

Front: Santa Claus, Yukon Cornelius; Back: Clarice, Abominable Snowman, Sam the Snowman, Rudolph

Dr. Dolittle®

A pair of small bean bags were issued as part of the press kit for the 1998 film *Dr. Dolittle*, starring Eddie Murphy. The entire kit consists of a water bowl and a pair of pins.

Item	W/1998	S/1999
Jake the tiger	$8.00	$8.00
Lucky the Dog	$8.00	$8.00

Jake, Lucky

E.T.®

This diminutive E.T. bean bag was reported to be available at Universal Studios.

Item	S/1999
E.T.	$9.00

Felix the Cat®

The old-time favorite cartoon character Felix the Cat was made very nicely into bean bag form.

Felix—Valentine's, Skidoo, Felix

Item	W/1998	S/1999
Felix	$10.00	$10.00
Felix, Valentine's, heart sewn on chest	$12.00	$12.00
Skidoo	$10.00	$8.00

Ferngully Batty Toy®

This mail-in offer was available on packages of the *Ferngully 2: The Magical Rescue* movie.

Item	W/1998	S/1999
Bat (R)	$12.00	$12.00

Flipper®

Flipper, the dolphin from the movie *Flipper*, was issued in bean bag form. Hard to find, this one was found on eBay. It's made by Toy Biz, Inc., and has a 1996 date on it.

Item	S/1999
Flipper	$9.00

For Pete's Sake®

Pete, the dog from *The Little Rascals,* was a bean bag premium for buying the movie *For Pete's Sake.*

Item	S/1999
Pete	$20.00

Gremlins 2®

These cute Gizmos from *Gremlins 2* were produced for the Japanese market by Jun Planning. Licensed by Warner Brothers and dated 1996. Hard to find.

Item	S/1999
Gizmo, blue	$20.00
Gizmo, brown	$20.00
Gizmo, purple	$20.00

Kratts' Creatures®

From the lively PBS show *Kratts' Creatures,* a dozen bean bags in display boxes were made in 1997. Nine of these were found at a close-out store.

Item	S/1999
Armadillo	$5.00
Bandicoot	$5.00
Beaver	$5.00
Flying Squirrel	$5.00
Hammerhead Bat	$5.00
Hippo	$5.00
Lizard	$5.00
Octopus	$5.00
Platypus	$5.00
Sloth	$5.00
Warthog	$5.00
Yak	$5.00

Hammerhead Bat, Warthog, Sloth

Octopus, Hippopotamus, Platypus

Beaver, Armadillo, Bandicoot

The Land Before Time®

No less than five movies have been made for this animated dinosaur adventure. The bean bags are large, sold in display boxes, and made by Equity Toys.

Item	S/1999
Cera	$9.00
Chomper	$9.00
Ducky	$9.00
Littlefoot	$9.00
Petrie	$9.00
Spike	$9.00

Littlefoot, Petrie, Cera

Spike, Chomper, Ducky

Lion King II: Simba's Pride® (Mattel)

Boxed sets of three characters from the Disney movie
Simba's Pride were produced by Mattel. Great for kids
and collectors.

Timon, Kiara, Pumbaa, Nuka, Kovu, Vitani

Item	S/1999
Timon, Kiara, Pumbaa	$12.00
Nuka, Kovu, Vitani	$12.00

Mickey for Kids Bean Bags® (Mattel)

Pluto, Goofy, Mickey, Minnie, Donald, Daisy

Item	S/1999
Daisy	$5.00
Donald	$5.00
Goofy	$5.00
Mickey	$5.00
Minnie	$5.00
Pluto	$5.00

Mr. Bill and Friends®

Fans of the old *Saturday Night Live* will recognize these characters. This set was purchased through a TV shopping network.

Item	S/1999
Mr. Bill	$6.00
Sluggo	$6.00
Spot	$6.00

Sluggo, Spot, Mr. Bill

Muppet Babies®

These cute Muppet Baby characters were found at a local close-out store. Before then, I'd never heard of them. Since then, I've never seen them again!

Miss Piggy, Gonzo, Animal

Item	S/1999
Animal	$6.00
Gonzo	$6.00
Kermit	$6.00
Miss Piggy	$6.00

New Zoo Revue®

From the children's show *The New Zoo Revue*.

Item	S/1999
Freddy the Frog	$7.00

Freddy the Frog

Nickelodeon Rugrats Bean Bags®

The highly popular Nickelodeon cartoon "Rugrats" have seen several sets of bean bags produced thus far. Spike the Dog is listed on the Play-By-Play "head" bean bag hang-tags as being part of that set.

Applause Set: Spike, Tommy, Chuckie, Angelica, Reptar

Blockbuster Set: Chuckie, Angelica, Spike, Lil, Phil, Tommy

Item	W/1998	S/1999
Rugrats (Applause)		
Angela	$6.00	$6.00
Chuckie	$6.00	$6.00
Reptar the dinosaur	$6.00	$6.00
Spike the dog	$6.00	$6.00
Tommy	$6.00	$6.00
Rugrats (Blockbuster Exclusives)		
Angela	n/a	$6.00
Chuckie	n/a	$6.00
Lil	n/a	$6.00
Phil	n/a	$6.00
Spike	n/a	$6.00
Tommy	n/a	$6.00
Holiday Rugrats Bean Bag Friends (Mattel)		
Angelica	$8.00	$8.00
Chuckie	$8.00	$8.00
Spike the dog	$8.00	$8.00
Tommy	$8.00	$8.00
Play-By-Play Rugrats Bean Bags		
Angelica	$5.00	$5.00
Chuckie	$5.00	$5.00
Tommy	$5.00	$5.00

Holiday Set: Chuckie, Angelica, Spike, and Tommy on furniture by Lillian Vernon

Play-By-Play Set: Angelica, Chuckie, Tommy

Noddy Cartoon®

"Golly" is a character from the British Broadcasting Company TV show *Noddy*. Golly is superbly manufactured by The Velveteen Bean Bear Company. Very hard to find. The Girl Golly was found in an on-line auction and has tags that say "A D.S.N. Quality Product." Both are made in England.

Golly   Girl Golly

Item	W/1998	S/1999
Golly	$25.00	$30.00
Girl Golly	n/a	$22.00

Sesame Street Beans®

Tyco issued 24 different Sesame Street Beans characters (some from the second set of 12 are not easy to find). Fisher-Price released a Sesame Street Beans three-character boxed set for Easter 1999, with the characters sporting bunny ears.

Top: Baby Bear, Telly, Grover, Guy Smiley, Benny Rabbit, Sherlock Hemlock, Twiddle Bug, Snuffleupagus;
Middle: Rubber Duckie, The Count, Ernie, Oscar the Grouch, Betty Lou, Bert, Mumford, Barkley;
Bottom: Honker, Elmo, Cookie Monster, Big Bird, Rosita, Zoe, Natasha, Herry Monster

Item	W/1998	S/1999
Tyco Sesame Street Beans		
Baby Bear	$6.00	$5.00
Barkley	$9.00	$10.00
Benny Rabbit	$8.00	$7.00
Bert	$7.00	$5.00
Betty Lou	$6.00	$5.00
Big Bird	$6.00	$5.00
Cookie Monster	$8.00	$5.00
The Count	$6.00	$5.00

Elmo	$6.00	$5.00
Ernie	$6.00	$5.00
Grover	$6.00	$5.00
Guy Smiley	$8.00	$10.00
Herry Monster	$8.00	$5.00
Honker, green	$6.00	$8.00
Honker, purple	$6.00	$5.00
Mumford	$8.00	$5.00
Natasha	$9.00	$14.00
Oscar	$8.00	$5.00
Rosita	$9.00	$15.00
Rubber Duckie	$6.00	$5.00
Sherlock Hemlock	$8.00	$8.00
Snuffleupagus	$9.00	$6.00
Telly Monster	$6.00	$5.00
Twiddle Bug	$9.00	$12.00
Zoe	$6.00	$5.00

Fisher-Price Sesame Street Beans
Elmo, Big Bird, Cookie
   Monster in boxed set   n/a $12.00

Honker—purple, green

Sesame Street Beans
Boxed Set

Snowden & Friends®

Sold exclusively at Target stores over the 1997 and 1998
holiday seasons, these sets are based on the characters
from the animated cartoon, *Snowden*. The Raggedy Ann
and Andy bean bags are highly sought.

Item	S/1999
1997 Snowden	
Redbird	$9.00
Snowden the Snowman	$9.00
1998 Snowden	
Bunny	$4.00
Deer	$4.00
Gosling	$4.00
Mouse	$4.00
Raccoon	$4.00
Raggedy Ann	$8.00
Raggedy Andy	$8.00
Redbird	$4.00
Snowden the Snowman	$4.00

Front: Raccoon,
Snowden, Mouse,
Gosling, Bunny, Deer;
Back: Raggedy Ann,
Raggedy Andy, Redbird

Spice Girls Bean Bag Dolls®

Made by The Idea Factory, these very cute bean bag dolls are great likenesses to their human counterparts. This set is popular among the pre-teen girls who not only love bean bags, but are wild about the pop-sensations, The Spice Girls. Each doll has a "Girl Power" hang-tag message and autograph from the Spice Girl depicted.

Item	S/1999
Baby (Emma Bunton)	$9.00
Posh (Victoria Adams)	$9.00
Scary (Melanie Brown)	$9.00
Sporty (Melanie C.)	$9.00

Scary, Sporty, Baby, Posh

Baby, Sporty, Scary, Posh

Star Trek Alien Beans®

Another set by The Idea Factory, these are very cool bean bags featuring favorite aliens from the *Star Trek* series. A total of 50,000 of each will be produced, and each has a numbered hang-tag indicating authenticity, history, and date of introduction. These are very popular among bean bag collectors and Trekkies alike. Now, beam me over some!

Item	S/1999
Andorian	$8.00
Ferengi	$8.00
Gorn	$8.00
Klingon Targ	$8.00
Mugato	$8.00
Vulcan	$8.00

Star Wars Buddies®

The famous characters from one of the most famous movies of all time make for a great set of bean bags.

Top: Jabba the Hutt, Jawa, Max Rebo, C-3PO; Bottom: Salacious Crumb, Chewbacca with brown sash, Wicket, R2-D2

Item	W/1998	S/1999
C-3PO	$8.00	$10.00
Chewbacca (1999)	n/a	n/a
Chewbacca with black sash	$8.00	$15.00
Chewbacca with brown sash	$14.00	$12.00
Figrin D'an	$12.00	$11.00
Darth Vader (1999)	n/a	n/a
Jabba the Hutt	$8.00	$8.00
Jawa	$8.00	$10.00
Max Rebo	$8.00	$8.00
R2-D2	$8.00	$8.00
Salacious Crumb	$8.00	$9.00
Stormtrooper (1999)	n/a	n/a
Wampa	$13.00	$10.00
Wicket the Ewok	$10.00	$10.00
Yoda	$14.00	$22.00

Figrin D'an, Wampa, Yoda

Chewbacca with black sash

Teletubbies®

Teletubbies, a British children's show, has taken United States by storm. Three bean bag sets have been produced so far. All three are well done.

Eden Set: Tinky-Winky, Dipsy, Laa-Laa, Po

Item	W/1998	S/1999
Eden		
Dipsy	n/a	$10.00
Laa-Laa	n/a	$10.00
Po	n/a	$10.00
Tinky-Winky	n/a	$10.00
Golden Bear		
Dipsy	$15.00	$10.00
Laa-Laa	$15.00	$10.00
Po	$15.00	$10.00
Tinky-Winky	$15.00	$10.00
Playskool		
Dipsy	$8.00	$6.00
Laa-Laa	$8.00	$6.00
Po	$8.00	$6.00
Tinky-Winky	$8.00	$6.00

Golden Bear Set: Tinky-Winky, Dipsy, Laa-Laa, Po

Playskool Set: Tinky-Winky, Dipsy, Laa-Laa, Po

Toy Story Mini Buddies® (Thinkaway Toys)

This five-piece set from Thinkaway Toys was produced in great quantities in 1998.

Item	W/1998	S/1999
Alien	$5.00	$4.00
Buzz Lightyear	$5.00	$4.00
Hamm the pig	$6.00	$4.00
Rex the dinosaur	$6.00	$4.00
Woody	$5.00	$4.00

Front: Buzz Lightyear, Alien, Woody; Back: Rex, Hamm

Wallace & Gromit®

This award-winning British clay-animation show has seen several sets made. PBS often airs these programs. The show is about an inventor named Wallace and his dog Gromit.

Item	S/1999
Gift set (England)	
Gromit the Dog and Shaun the Sheep	$20.00
Set (England)	
Feathers the Penguin	$10.00
Gromit the Dog	$10.00
Shaun the Sheep	$10.00
Wallace	$10.00
Set (Gund)	
Feathers the Penguin	$6.00
Gromit the Dog	$6.00
Shaun the Sheep	$6.00
Wallace	$6.00

Gift Set: Gromit, Shaun

Wishbone®

Denny's promotion included two Wishbone (of the PBS children's show) bean bags. The Dr. Jeckyl and Equity toy versions were available at convenience and mass-market stores.

Wishbone—lying down (Denny's), sitting, Dr. Jeckyl, lying down (Equity Toys)

Item	W/1998	S/1999
Wishbone, Dr. Jeckyl	n/a	$6.00
Wishbone, lying down (Denny's)	$7.00	$8.00
Wishbone, lying down (Equity Toys)	n/a	$5.00
Wishbone, sitting (Denny's)	$7.00	$8.00

Wizard of Oz® (Merry-O Collection)

This set of ten hard-faced bean bags is rather nice. The set was available in November 1998 and seemed to sell out quickly. Made by Trevco.

Item	S/1999
Ballerina Munchkin	$5.00
Dorothy	$5.00
Glinda	$5.00
Lion	$5.00
Lollipop Munchkin	$5.00
Scarecrow	$5.00
Tin Man	$5.00
Toto	$5.00
Wicked Witch	$5.00
Winged Monkey	$5.00

Toto and Dorothy on furniture by Lillian Vernon

Other
Major Bean
Bag Lines

Avon®

These excellent sets from Avon are worth adding to your collection. Check with your local Avon representative for information about ordering them.

Avon 1: Bernard the Bear; Avon 2: Dapper the Dinosaur; Avon 3: Juggler the Seal; Avon 4: Jumbo the Elephant; Avon 5: Lenny the Leopard; Avon 6: Mozzarella the Mouse; Avon 7: Rumply the Sharpei; Avon 8: Skips the Puppy; Avon 9: Stretch the Giraffe; Avon 10: Zoe the Zebra.

Item	W/1998	S/1999
Full O' Beans Set #1 (R)		
Bernard the Bear	$6.00	$9.00
Dapper the Dinosaur	$6.00	$6.00
Juggler the Seal	$6.00	$6.00
Jumbo the Elephant	$7.00	$6.00
Lenny the Leopard	$6.00	$6.00
Mozzarella the Mouse	$6.00	$6.00
Rumply the Sharpei	$9.00	$9.00
Skips the Puppy	$8.00	$7.00
Stretch the Giraffe	$8.00	$7.00
Zoe the Zebra	$20.00	$18.00
Full O' Beans Set #2 (Birthstone)		
January/Flipper the Penguin (garnet)	n/a	$6.00
February/Cody the Bear (amethyst)	n/a	$6.00
March/Tad the Frog (aquamarine)	n/a	$6.00
April/Twinks the Bunny (diamond)	n/a	$6.00
May/Shelly the Turtle (emerald)	n/a	$6.00
June/Coconut the Monkey (alexandrite)	n/a	$6.00
July/Rocky the Rhino (ruby)	n/a	$6.00
August/Tabitha the Cat (peridot)	n/a	$6.00
September/Dune the Camel (sapphire)	n/a	$6.00
October/Trumpet the Elephant (rose zircon)	n/a	$6.00
November/Scout the Terrier (topaz)	n/a	$6.00
December/Spruce the Moose (blue zircon)	n/a	$6.00
Giggle Bean Pals		
Big Bird	n/a	$10.00
Cookie Monster	n/a	$10.00
Elmo	n/a	$10.00

Beanie Kids®

Floppy the cat, Angel the bear, Tutu the bear, Blaze the dog

The well-crafted Beanie Kids are Australia's entrant into the world of bean bag plush. Teddy Bear collectors will especially enjoy tracking down all the bears in this set. Reportedly, some Beanie Kids were very limited, such as Blaze, Goldy, and Jade (less than 2,200). Collector information is available at: http://www.beaniekids.com

Item	W/1998	S/1999
Amber the bear (R)	$7.00	$8.00
Angel the bear	$7.00	$7.00
Berry the bear	n/a	$7.00
Bernard the bear, red ribbon (R)	$10.00	$20.00
Bernard the bear, tartan ribbon (R)	$10.00	$30.00
Blackie the black bear	$12.00	$7.00
Blaze the dog (R)	$10.00	$65.00
Bluey the bear	$12.00	$7.00
Bongo the bear	$7.00	$7.00
Boo the ghost (R)	$12.00	$8.00
Boris the brontosaurus (R)	$9.00	$8.00
Buttercup the cow	$8.00	$7.00
Camilla the gorilla	$8.00	$7.00
Chi Chi the panda	$10.00	$7.00
Chip the monkey	$7.00	$7.00
Chuckie the chook (R)	$10.00	$27.00
Claws the crab (R)	$10.00	$8.00
Croaker the frog (R)	$7.00	$18.00
Curly the pig	$7.00	$7.00
Daisy the cow	n/a	$7.00
Deborah the zebra (R)	$10.00	$8.00
Fizz the bear	n/a	$7.00
Flame the little devil (R)	$13.00	$7.00
Floppy the cat (R)	$7.00	$10.00
Free the butterfly	n/a	$7.00
Gerome the giraffe	n/a	$7.00
Gills the tropical fish (R)	$10.00	$8.00
Goldy the bear (R)	$10.00	$200.00
Hippy the bear	$7.00	$7.00
Honey the bee	$10.00	$7.00
Howard the hippo (R)	$7.00	$8.00
Jade the green bear (R)	$10.00	$200.00
Jaffa the orange/ black bear	$12.00	$7.00
Jessie the rabbit (R)	$8.00	$7.00
Juliet the bear	n/a	$7.00
Kiwi the New Zealand bear	$12.00	$10.00
Kringle the Christmas bear	n/a	$15.00
Legend the unicorn	n/a	$7.00
Legs the redback spider	$12.00	$7.00

Item	W/1998	S/1999
Lenny the leopard	$7.00	$7.00
Leo the lion	$7.00	$7.00
Lilly the frog (R)	$7.00	$12.00
Lizzie the frill neck lizard (R)	$10.00	$8.00
Love the brown bear, red ribbon (R)	$7.00	$8.00
Love the brown bear, tartan ribbon (R)	$10.00	$50.00+
Love the tan bear, red ribbon (R)	$10.00	$50.00+
Love the tan bear, tartan ribbon (R)	$10.00	$50.00+
Lumpy the camel	n/a	$7.00
Matilda the bear, red ribbon (R)	$18.00	$50.00+
Matilda the bear, tartan ribbon (R)	$7.00	$8.00
Matt the bat	$12.00	$7.00
Minty the bear	n/a	$7.00
Moo the cow, talking	$12.00	$10.00
Nellie the elephant (R)	$16.00	$8.00
Neptune the sea horse (R)	$10.00	$8.00
Nicholas the tan bear	$10.00	$7.00
Noel the Christmas bear (R)	$10.00	$8.00
Oink the pig, talking (R)	$12.00	$10.00
Oliver the bear	n/a	$7.00
Ozzie the Aussie bear	$12.00	$10.00
Percy the penguin	n/a	$7.00
Polly the polar bear	$10.00	$7.00
Pop the bear	n/a	$7.00
Proud the bear	n/a	$7.00
Ribbit the frog (R)	$10.00	$10.00
Romeo the bear	n/a	$7.00
Rover the red nose reindog (R)	$10.00	$8.00
Ruby the bear	$7.00	$7.00
Rusty the cat (R)	$10.00	$10.00
Sadie the bear	n/a	$7.00
Sammy the punk (R)	$10.00	$25.00
Slinky the seal (R)	$8.00	$8.00
Smiley the bear (R)	$10.00	$8.00
Sooty the lamb	n/a	$7.00
Spice the bear	n/a	$7.00
Spike the bullie	$8.00	$7.00
Splash the dolphin	$12.00	$7.00
Spot the dog	$22.00	$7.00
Spud the bullie (R)	$8.00	$8.00
Star the bear	n/a	$7.00
Sunny the dog (R)	$7.00	$50.00+
Tango the dog (R)	$10.00	$50.00+
Tingle the bear	n/a	$7.00
Toby the pony (R)	$10.00	$8.00
Tooks the toucan	n/a	$7.00
Tuffy the cat (R)	$7.00	$8.00
TuTu the bear	$7.00	$7.00
Twinkle the bear	n/a	$7.00
Violet the bear (R)	$7.00	$8.00

Item	W/1998	S/1999
Waddle the duck	n/a	$7.00
Wallace the walrus	n/a	$7.00
Webster the duck (R)	$10.00	$18.00
Willie the orca whale	$10.00	$7.00
Woof the dog, talking (R)	$12.00	$10.00
Zap the bear	n/a	$7.00
Zelda the witch	$12.00	$7.00

Celebrity Bears®

Issued by JC Bears, these bears are dynamite! Each bear has celebrity characteristics providing hints as to whom the bear is modeled after. The company's website offers clues to up-coming bears and announces its retirements: http://www.celebritybears.com

Item	S/1999
#1. Arnold Schwarzenegger	$9.00
#2. Rosie O'Donnell	$12.00
#3. Garth Brooks	$10.00
#4. Will Smith (R)	$10.00
#5. Mel Gibson	$8.00
#6. Elvis	$11.00
#7. Hulk Hogan (R)	$8.00
#8. Ginger Spice	$9.00
#9. Michael Jordan (R)	$18.00
#10. Mariah Carey	$7.00
#11. Leonardo DiCaprio (R)	$9.00
#12. Tiger Woods	$9.00
#14. Sylvester Stallone	$7.00
#15. Dennis Rodman	$8.00
#16. Shania Twain	$8.00
#17. Hanson	$7.00
#18. Kate Winslet	$9.00
#19. Indiana Jones	$8.00
#20. Martha Stewart	$9.00
#21. Tim Allen	$7.00
#22. Whoopi Goldberg	$9.00
#23. George Clooney	$8.00
#24. Jeff Gordon	$15.00
#25. Mark McGwire	$11.00
#26. Cher	$9.00

Front: #1, #2, #3;
Back: #4, #5, #6

Front: #14, #15;
Back: #16, #17

Front: #7, #8, #9; Back: #10, #11, #12

Cherished Teddies®

A new line of bears from Enesco, the Cherished Teddies bean bags are cute and collectible. Be sure to check out Enesco's website at: http://www.enesco.com

Bear with red heart, Jackie, Sara

Item	S/1999
Ava, bright pink bow	$10.00
Jackie, light green and white bow	$7.00
Karen, peach and white bow	$7.00
Sara, light purple bow	$7.00
Bear, red heart	$12.00
Bear, "Best Friends" T-shirt	$6.00
Bear, "Hug Me" T-shirt	$6.00
Bear, "Love Me" T-shirt	$6.00
Bear, "Miss You" T-shirt	$6.00
Bear, "Need You" T-shirt	$6.00
Bear, "Smile" T-shirt	$6.00

Bears—Top: Hug Me, Miss You, Love Me; Bottom: Smile, Best Friends, Need You

Classic Collecticritters®

Another company producing "celebrity" bean bags, Classic Collecticritters makes bears that have names and characteristics related to popular personalities. Most are limited to 10,000, with a few less than that. The company website is at: http://www.collecticritters.com

Item	S/1999
Classic Bear Series I	
The Dukester	$15.00
Frankie	$14.00
The King	$20.00
Lucy	$32.00
Marilyn	$20.00
Classic Bear Series II	
Bryant	$8.00
Harmony	$24.00
Love	$12.00
Rocky	$8.00
Shirley	$13.00
Jewel Series	
Amber	$12.00
Emerald	$11.00
Ruby	$12.00
Topaz	$10.00
Turquoise	$12.00

Classic Bear Series I

Promo Bear Series 1
Homer $52.00

Promo Bears Series II
Hawaii $24.00
T.D. $24.00

Red, White and Blue Series
Blue Senator $9.00
Red Senator $9.00
White Senator $9.00

Ronald McDonald Series
White Bear, Ronald McDonald Charities
  of Southern California $10.00
White Bear, Camp Ronald McDonald
  for Good Times $10.00
Blue Bear, Loma Linda
  Ronald McDonald House $10.00
Red Bear, Los Angeles Ronald
  McDonald House for Good Times $10.00
Yellow Bear, Orange County
  Ronald McDonald House $10.00

Signature Series
Joe Montana #3, green jersey $14.00
Joe Montana #3, green jersey,
  autographed   n/a
Joe Montana #3, white jersey $14.00
Joe Montana #3, white jersey,
  autographed   n/a
Joe Montana #16, red jersey $14.00
Joe Montana #16, red jersey,
  autographed   n/a
Joe Montana #16, white jersey $14.00
Joe Montana #16, white jersey,
  autographed   n/a
Joe Montana #19, red jersey $14.00
Joe Montana #19, red jersey,
  autographed   n/a
Joe Montana, "promo" #1   n/a
Joe Montana, "promo" #2   n/a
Tony Gwynn #19, autographed   n/a
Tony Gwynn, "promo"   n/a

Surprise Bear
Dunk, "promo"   n/a
Texas, "promo"   n/a

VIP Series

Jackie, Edition 1, blue	$30.00
Jackie, Edition 2, burgundy	$18.00
The Senator, Edition 1, gray	$32.00
The Senator, Edition 2, white	$20.00

Y2K Millennium Series

Y, White Bear	$22.00
2, Gray Bear	$22.00
K, Black Bear	$22.00

Classy Tassy's Bears®

Peaches Gorja, Rip Van Twinkle

One of the new entrants into the bean-bag bear market is Classy Tassy's Bears. These bean bags, which represent states, are super quality. Weighing about a half-pound each, they are some of the heaviest bean bags around. Their rigid plastic hang-tags are 2-D Flics that show different images when turned. The company intends to produce a bean bag bear for each state, plus the District of Columbia. One green-and-white pajama Rip Van Twinkle was produced for every 11 red-and-white pajama versions. Maureena Marina will have her flags changed from time to time. The company's website is at: http://www.classytassy.com/index.htm

Item	S/1999
Abbey Applelet (New York)	$10.00
Blu Jean (Louisiana)	$10.00
Dallas Starr (Texas)	$10.00
Felicia Flamingo (Florida)	$10.00
J.R. Casino (USA)	$10.00
Kiddie Jubilee (Birthday)	$10.00
Maureena Marina (New Jersey)	$10.00
Ms. Society (California)	$10.00
Oops Bartholomeu, green (North Carolina)	n/a
Oops Bartholomeu, orange (North Carolina)	n/a
Oops Bartholomeu, pink (North Carolina)	n/a
Orchid Maui (Hawaii)	$10.00
Peaches Gorja (Georgia)	$10.00
Riblet Montgomery (Ohio)	$10.00
Rip Van Twinkle, red/white pajamas (Wyoming)	$10.00
Rip Van Twinkle, green/white pajamas (Wyoming)	$20.00
Terri Tanasi (Tennessee)	$10.00
Wolfy Wolverine (Michigan)	$10.00

Coca-Cola Bean Bag Plush®

Combine the power of the world's No. 1 soft drink with cute characters in bean bag form and what do you get? Cola bean bag plush sets that are very popular among bean bag collectors and Coca-Cola collectors.

The new Coca-Cola International Bean Bag collection was introduced this year. Starting in April, the first set of 10 characters was simultaneously introduced and retired on the same day. Ten more were released in June and August, and additional sets of 10 will become availabe in October and December. Each of the 50 cuddly animal characters in the 1999 collection represents a country where Coke is served. Each has its own name and carries its national flag and a bottle of Coca-Cola. A high-security holographic hang-tag is encased in a special bottle cap-shaped clear protector which guarantees authenticity. A special 51st critter of the Coca-Cola International Bean Bag Collection—a really neat-looking buffalo named Totonca— is for members of the Collector's Society only. Some of the characters from this line will have different names in the Canadian market, due to some names already being trademarked there (the bean bags are the same, only the names change). To locate dealers in Canada, contact the Frederick Dickson Company in Toronto at (416) 751-4685. Coca-Cola Bean Bag Plush is made by Cavanagh, producer of several fine lines of bean bag collectibles. Check out Cavanagh's website at: http://www.cavanaghgrp.com

Item	W/1998	S/1999
Spring 1997 (R)		
Penguin, delivery cap, #108	$10.00	$14.00
Polar Bear, baseball cap, #111	$10.00	$14.00
Polar Bear, pink bow, #110	$10.00	$14.00
Polar Bear, T-shirt, #112	$10.00	$14.00
Polar Bear, holding bottle, #109	$10.00	$14.00
Seal, baseball cap, #107	$10.00	$14.00

Item

Coke—Spring 1997

	W/1998	S/1999
Holiday 1997 (R)		
Penguin, snowflake cap, #103	$10.00	$12.00
Polar Bear, plaid bow, #105	$10.00	$12.00
Polar Bear, red bow, #106	$10.00	$12.00
Polar Bear, snowflake cap, #104	$10.00	$12.00
Seal, scarf, #101	$10.00	$12.00
Seal, snowflake cap, #102	$10.00	$12.00

Coke—Holiday 1997

	W/1998	S/1999
Heritage I, 1998 (R)		
Coca-Cola Can, #132	$9.00	$10.00
Polar Bear, driver's cap, #140	$9.00	$10.00
Polar Bear, sweater, #116	$9.00	$10.00
Reindeer, shirt, #133	$9.00	$10.00
Seal, ski cap, #114	$9.00	$10.00
Walrus, bottle and scarf, #124	$9.00	$10.00

Coke—Heritage 1

	W/1998	S/1999
Heritage II, 1998 (R)		
Penguin, green vest, #172	$7.00	$9.00
Polar Bear, cap and scarf, #167	$7.00	$9.00
Polar Bear, blue ski cap, #169	$7.00	$9.00
Polar Bear, soda fountain clothes, #171	$7.00	$9.00

Item	W/1998	S/1999
Reindeer, colorful vest and beanie hat, #168	$7.00	$9.00
Seal, delivery outfit, #170	$7.00	$9.00

Coke—Heritage II

Everyday, 1998 (R)

Husky, bottle, #136	$7.00	$8.00
Penguin, chef's hat, #127	$7.00	$8.00
Polar Bear, argyle shirt, #131	$7.00	$8.00
Reindeer, bottle, #152	$7.00	$8.00
Walrus, bottle, #135	$7.00	$8.00
Whale, bottle, #137	$7.00	$8.00

Coke—Everyday 1998

Winter, 1998 (R)

Penguin, snowflake scarf, #155	$7.00	$8.00
Polar Bear, red scarf, #120	$7.00	$8.00

Coke—Winter 1998

Item	W/1998	S/1999
Polar Bear, snowflake hat, #118	$7.00	$8.00
Reindeer, snowflake scarf, #142	$7.00	$8.00
Seal, green scarf, #123	$7.00	$8.00
Walrus, snowflake hat, #141	$7.00	$8.00

Sport, 1999

Item	W/1998	S/1999
Penguin, hockey, #263	n/a	$7.00
Polar Bear, baseball, #261	n/a	$7.00
Polar Bear, skiing, #265	n/a	$7.00
Polar Bear, golf, #264	n/a	$7.00
Polar Bear, football, #262	n/a	$7.00
Seal, soccer, #266	n/a	$7.00

Everyday, 1999

Item	W/1998	S/1999
Penguin, vest, #202	n/a	$7.00
Polar Bear, shirt, #200	n/a	$7.00
Polar Bear, baseball cap, #199	n/a	$7.00
Polar Bear, scarf, #201	n/a	$7.00
Seal, baseball cap, #204	n/a	$7.00
Seal, scarf, #203	n/a	$7.00

Winter, 1999

Item	W/1998	S/1999
Penguin, green cap, #205	n/a	$7.00
Polar Bear, snowflake hat and vest, #208	n/a	$7.00
Polar Bear, striped hat and scarf, #206	n/a	$7.00
Polar Bear, striped shirt and scarf, #209	n/a	$7.00
Seal, scarf and red hat, #210	n/a	$7.00
Seal, vest and green cap, #207	n/a	$7.00

Item	W/1998	S/1999
Blockbuster Exclusives, 1997 (R)		
Penguin, snowflake cap, #148	$14.00	$32.00
Polar Bear, driver's cap, #146	$14.00	$32.00
Polar Bear, green bow, #144	$14.00	$32.00
Polar Bear, vest, #149	$14.00	$32.00
Seal, scarf, #145	$14.00	$32.00
Seal, snowflake cap, #147	$14.00	$32.00

Coca-Cola Collector's Society

Polar Bear, sweater, LE 1998, #151 (R)
$22.00 $25.00
Polar Bear, polka-dot collar, LE 1999, #126
n/a $15.00

#126, #151

Coca-Cola Convention Exclusives (R)

Item	W/1998	S/1999
Frog, Coca-Cola convention shirt (LE 400)	$80.00	$250.00
Moose, Coca-Cola convention shirt (LE 144)	$90.00	$345.00

Coca-Cola Store Exclusives

Polar Bear, Collector Classic T-shirt, #184
n/a $18.00
Polar Bear, city specific store on shirt (Atlanta or Las Vegas), #191
n/a $15.00
Polar Bear, red scarf, #159
$20.00 $20.00
Seal, T-Shirt, #158
$20.00 $20.00

Polar Bear dressed in Collector Classic T-Shirt, #184

Gift Creation Concept Retailer Exclusive

Item	W/1998	S/1999
Polar Bear, hat and vest, #166	n/a	$15.00
Polar Bear, red romper, #267	n/a	$20.00

Manchu Wok Restaurants Exclusive

Item	W/1998	S/1999
Bear, Chinese shirt, #177	n/a	$12.00

Item	W/1998	S/1999

Media Play Exclusives, 1998

Polar Bear, shirt, #161
| | n/a | $15.00 |

Polar Bear, holiday scarf, #163
| | n/a | $15.00 |

Reindeer, holiday shirt, #162
| | n/a | $15.00 |

Seal, holiday cap, #164
| | n/a | $15.00 |

Coke—Media Play

Musicland Exclusive (R)
Polar Bear, snowflake
cap, #113 $25.00 $30.00

Parade of Gifts Exclusive
Polar Bear,
trademark vest, #165   n/a $10.00

White's Kissing Bears (R)

Polar Bear, green bow, #153
(LE 15,000)
     $20.00 $22.00

Polar Bear, jumper (LE 15,000)
     n/a $12.00

Polar Bear, red and white scarf,
#154 (LE 15,000)
     $20.00 $22.00

Polar Bear, red bow (LE 15,000)
     n/a $12.00

Coke—Kissing

World of Coca-Cola Exclusives
| Polar Bear, black tux, red tie, #193 | n/a | $15.00 |
| Polar Bear, red bow tie, red bow, #194 | n/a | $15.00 |

Australia Exclusive, 1998 (Hungry Jacks)
| Polar Bear, female, bow | n/a | $20.00 |
| Polar Bear, male, scarf | n/a | $20.00 |

Australia Exclusive, 1999
Bunny, ball	n/a	$12.00
Bunny, scarf	n/a	$12.00
Bunny, shirt	n/a	$12.00
Bunny, shorts	n/a	$12.00

1999 Coca-Cola International Bean Bag Collection
1. Reegle the Bald Eagle, United States, #211		$8.00
2. Clomp the Elephant, Kenya, #217		$8.00
3. Masa the Lion, Mozambique, #219		$8.00
4. Rilly the Gorilla, Rwanda, #218		$8.00
5. Dover the Bulldog, England, #213		$8.00
6. Strudel the French Poodle, France, #214		$8.00

Item	S/1999
7. Quala the Koala Bear, Australia, #220	$8.00
8. Curry the Bengal Tiger, India, #216	$8.00
9. Toolu the Toucan, Honduras, #212	$8.00
10. Toro the Bull, Spain, #215	$8.00
11. Can Can the Pelican, Cuba, #221	$8.00
12. Baltic the Reindeer, Sweden, #222	$8.00
13. Paco the Iguana, Mexico, #223	$8.00
14. Rifraff the Giraffe, Somalia, #224	$8.00
15. Croon the Baboon, Pakistan, #225	$8.00
16. Salty the Green Sea Turtle, Bahamas, #226	$8.00
17. Vaca the Long Horn Cow, Argentina, #227	$8.00
18. Zongshi the Panda Bear, China, #228	$8.00
19. Barrot the Parrot, Brazil, #229	$8.00
20. Fannie the Red Fox, Germany, #230	$8.00
21. Taps the Tapir, Venezuela, #231	$8.00
22. Rhiny the Black Rhinoceros, Tanzania, #232	$8.00
23. Gormund the Moose, Canada, #233	$8.00
24. Lors the Wild Boar, Italy, #234	$8.00
25. Barris the Brown Bear, Russia, #235	$8.00
26. Waks the Yak, Nepal, #236	$8.00
27. Key Key the Snow Monkey, Japan, #237	$8.00
28. Ramel the Camel, Egypt, #238	$8.00
29. Pock the Peacock, Sri Lanka, #239	$8.00
30. Badgey the Badger, Czech Republic, #240	$8.00
31. Topus the Zebra, Nigeria, #241	$8.00
32. Waller the Walrus, Greenland, #242	$8.00
33. Laffs the Llama, Bolivia, #243	$8.00
34. Woolsy the Sheep, Ireland, #244	$8.00
35. Crunch the Crocodile, Sudan, #245	$8.00
36. Howls the Wolf, Romania, #246	$8.00
37. Orany the Orangutan, Singapore, #247	$8.00
38. Ardie the Aardvark, Niger, #248	$8.00
39. Heetah the Cheetah, Namibia, #249	$8.00
40. Blubby the Pot Belly Pig, Vietnam, #250	$8.00
41. Hopps the Coki Frog, Puerto Rico, #251	$8.00
42. Peng the Penguin, Chile, #252	$8.00
43. Lochs the Rabbit, Scotland, #253	$8.00
44. Neppy the Proboscis Monkey, Thailand, #254	$8.00
45. Meeska the Hippopotamus, Zambia, #255	$8.00
46. Nardie the St. Bernard, Switzerland, #256	$8.00
47. Kelp the Kiwi, New Zealand, #257	$8.00

Item	S/1999
48. Oppy the Octopus, Greece, #258	$8.00
49. Streak the Jackal, Tunisia, #259	$8.00
50. Masha the Ostrich, South Africa, #260	$8.00
51. Totonca the Buffalo, US, #268, Collector's Society members only	n/a

Canadian CCIBBC with name changes

9. Toulu the Toucan, Honduras, #212	$8.00
20. After the Red Fox, Germany, #230	$8.00
22. Bello the Black Rhinoceros, Tanzania, #232	$8.00
25. Baris the Brown Bear, Russia, #235	$8.00
31. Zeb the Zebra, Nigeria, #241	$8.00
33. Loafer the Llama, Bolivia, #243	$8.00
34. Woolsey the Sheep, Ireland, #244	$8.00
36. Streak the Wolf, Romania, #246	$8.00
40. Bella the Pot Belly Pig, Vietnam, #250	$8.00
44. Popo the Proboscis Monkey, Thailand, #254	$8.00
45. Amos the Hippopotamus, Zambia, #255	$8.00
47. Wiki the Kiwi, New Zealand, #257	$8.00
48. Otto the Octopus, Greece, #258	$8.00
49. Kackel the Jackal, Tunisia, #259	$8.00
50. Stitch the Ostrich, South Africa, #260	$8.00

Eckerd®

This national chain drug store has offered many different bean bag sets. Several were produced by Dandee International Ltd.

Item	S/1999
Boo Bean (1997)	
Scareycrow the scarecrow	$5.00
Punkin the pumpkin	$5.00
Boo Beans (1998)	
Bagley the bag	$5.00
Brewster the pot	$5.00
Murray the mummy	$5.00
Cool Bugs (1999)	
Bright Bee	$5.00
Chatterbug	$5.00
Classhopper	$5.00
Wisefly	$5.00
Merry Beans (1998)	
Nutmeg	$5.00
Purty Poinsettia	$5.00
Snowman	$5.00

Shutterbugs (1999)

Digital	$5.00
Flash	$5.00
Focus	$5.00
Foto	$5.00
Redeye	$5.00
Rewind	$5.00
Tripod	$5.00
Zoom	$5.00

Nutmeg, Snowman,
Hopster, Chipper

Spring Beans (1999)

Bud the flower	$5.00
Chipper the duck	$5.00
Duffy the duck	$5.00
Flora the flower	$5.00
Hopster the bunny	$5.00
Sunnyside the egg	$5.00

Grateful Dead Bean Bears®

High in quality and visually appealing, these bean bag bears
are sure to make you smile. Look for the Delilah bear with-

Laminated
Tag

out the black pads on her hands. According
to the bean bears' maker, Liquid Blue, just
11,000 of this variation/error were made. It's
a very hard-to-find mistake. These bears
also sport a very special laminated full-color
tag with the bear's name, birth data, and a
"favorite tour memory" from a Grateful Dead
show road trip.

Althea, Bertha, Cassidy, Cosmic Charlie, Jack Straw

St. Stephen, Stagger Lee, Samson, Sugaree,
Tennessee Jed

Set I (1997)

Althea (R)	$14.00	$20.00
Bertha (R)	$9.00	$9.00
Cassidy (R)	$8.00	$9.00
Cosmic Charlie	$14.00	$10.00

Delilah, black pads on hands (R)	$20.00	$30.00
Delilah, without black pads on hands (R)	$50.00	$60.00
Jack Straw (R)	$12.00	$24.00
St. Stephen	$14.00	$15.00
Samson (R)	$10.00	$10.00
Stagger Lee (R)	$10.00	$10.00
Sugaree (R)	$20.00	$30.00
Tennessee Jed (R)	$16.00	$20.00

Delilah without blac paws, Delilah with black paws

Set II (1998)

Crazy Fingers	$12.00	$9.00
Dark Star	$14.00	$10.00
Daydream	$10.00	$9.00
Dupree	$10.00	$8.00
Franklin (R)	$8.00	$10.00
Irie (R)	$13.00	$11.00
Jerry	$24.00	$9.00
Peggy-O	$12.00	$8.00
Ripple	$13.00	$8.00
Sunshine	$10.00	$10.00

Top: Irie, Crazy Fingers, Ripple, Dark Star; Bottom: Jerry, Sunshine, Peggy-O, Daydream, Dupree, Franklin

Set III

Ashbury	n/a	$9.00
August West	n/a	$9.00
Blues Man	n/a	$9.00
China Cat	n/a	$9.00
Daisy	n/a	$9.00
Doodah Man	n/a	$9.00
Esau	n/a	$9.00
Foolish Heart	n/a	$9.00
Haight	n/a	$9.00
Pearly Baker	n/a	$9.00
Reuben	n/a	$9.00
Uncle Sam	n/a	$9.00

Daisy

Limited Edition
Black Peter
(LE 30,000) (R)   n/a $45.00

Black Peter

Gund Bean Bags®

Gund bean bags are catching on among collectors who have found these items not so easy to come across. Super quality and super cute, these bean bags are likely to be ones collectors will be looking for down the road. They cost a little more than other bean bags, but they do feature recognizable characters. Several of the lesser-known characters from the Dilbert line might be good buys, especially if Dilbert becomes the next big trend in comic strip collectibles.

Item	W/1998	S/1999
Animal Bean Bags		
Dahling the ostrich	$8.00	$8.00
Flash the frog, all green	$10.00	$8.00
Flash the frog, green with yellow belly	$10.00	$8.00
Flash the frog, green with light green belly	$8.00	$8.00
Mooky the walrus	$10.00	$9.00
Puddles the dog	$7.00	$7.00
Rainbow Racer the turtle	$7.00	$7.00
Slider the bear	$7.00	$7.00
Snuffy the bear, chocolate brown	$8.00	$8.00
Snuffy the bear, tan brown	$8.00	$8.00
Tender Teddy the bear, dark brown	$8.00	$8.00
Tinkle the inch worm	$7.00	$7.00
Classic Pooh		
Eeyore	$8.00	$8.00
Kanga	$8.00	$8.00
Piglet, grayish-green	$8.00	$8.00
Piglet, soft green	$8.00	$8.00
Tigger	$8.00	$8.00
Winnie-the-Pooh	$8.00	$8.00
Dilbert		
Alice	$16.00	$9.00
Boss	$8.00	$8.00
Catbert	$18.00	$9.00
Dilbert	$8.00	$8.00
Dogbert	$8.00	$8.00
Ratbert	$8.00	$8.00

Dahling, Mooky

Piglet, Kanga, Pooh, Eeyore, Tigger

Harley-Davidson Bean Bag Plush®

The Harley-Davidson Bean Bag Plush characters, first released in 1997, are still proving popular sellers in the Harley and bean bag collecting communities. Made by Cavanagh. Check out its website at: http://www.cavanagh-grp.com

Item	W/1998	S/1999
Set 1 (1997) (R)		
Big Twin bear	$10.00	$9.00
Motorhead bear	$10.00	$9.00
Punky hog	$10.00	$9.00
Racer hog	$10.00	$9.00
Rachet hog	$10.00	$9.00
Roamer bear	$10.00	$9.00

Top: Rachet; Middle: Punky, Racer; Bottom: Motorhead, Roamer, Big Twin

Set 2 (1998)		
Clutch Carbo hog	$8.00	$7.00
Evo bear	$8.00	$7.00
Fat Bob hog	$8.00	$7.00
Kickstart bear	$8.00	$7.00
Manifold Max bear	$8.00	$7.00
Spike bulldog	$8.00	$7.00

Top: Spike; Middle: Fat Bob, Clutch Carbo; Bottom: Evo, Max Manifold, Kickstart

Set 3 (1999)		
Boot Hill Bob pig	n/a	n/a
Bravo bear	n/a	n/a
Bubba raccoon	n/a	n/a
Tanker bulldog	n/a	n/a
Thunder bulldog	n/a	n/a
Tusk walrus	n/a	n/a

Top: Bubba; Bottom: Thunder, Tanker, Boot Hill Bob, Tusk, Bravo

Kissing Pair (White's Guide Exclusive)		
Baby Blue pig (LE 15,000)	$18.00	$10.00
Studs pig (LE 15,000)	$18.00	$10.00
Limited Edition		
Chopper the walrus	$22.00	$15.00
Tank the bear	n/a	$30.00
Rocky the raccoon	n/a	$22.00

Top: Studs, Baby Blue; Bottom: Tank, Chopper

Huggable Handfuls®

Front: Coco Leopard, Eloise Elephant, Lana Lamb; Back: Pamie Pig, Deena Duck, Amanda Panda, Lana Lamb, Lars Lion. Huggable Handfuls are pictured on Lillian Vernon bean bag animals' living room furniture.

These bean bag animals made by Lillian Vernon are extremely cute. There are neat accessories available for the Huggable Handfuls, as well. The bean bag furniture is adorable and very well made, and there is also a personalized over-door bean bag holder and a carrier available through their catalog. Check out the company's website at http://www.lillian vernon.com or call 800-505-2250 for more information or to order these superb bean bags and related products!

Item	S/1999
Amanda Panda	$4.00
Carla Cow	$4.00
Coco Leopard	$4.00
Deena Duck	$4.00
Eloise Elephant	$4.00
Lana Lamb	$4.00
Lars Lion	$4.00
Pamie Pig	$4.00

Limited Treasures®

Limited edition bean bags depict celebrities, holiday themes, and sports stars. These nice-quality bean bags, with holograms on their hang-tags to prevent counterfeiting, may become even more collectible down the road. All the bean bags (with the exception of the football characters) come packed in their own "treasure boxes." Limited Treasures has a website at: http://www.limitedtreasures.com

Item	S/1999
1st Issue (R)	
Elvis, blue	$27.00
Elvis, "test" bear	$45.00
Elvis, white "chase" bear	$70.00
Gordon	$25.00
Gordon, "test" bear	$45.00
Sam	$12.00
Sam, "test" bear	$30.00
Sherlock	$12.00
Sherlock, "test" bear	$20.00

Elvis in "Treasure" box

2nd Issue, Holiday Collection (R)	
Bear Claus	$5.00
Celebration, blue "chase" bear	$20.00
Celebration, gold "chase" bear	$75.00
Celebration, green "chase" bear	$20.00

Celebration, purple "chase" bear	$20.00
Celebration, white	$5.00
Heavenly Holly	$5.00
Peppermint	$5.00

Elvis, Gordon, Sam, Sherlock

3rd Issue, NFL Bears
"Premium Pro Bears" Series I (R)

Barry Sanders #20	$7.00
Barry Sanders #20, white "chase" bear	$20.00
Brett Favre #4	$7.00
Brett Favre #4, "test" bear	$15.00
Brett Favre #4, white "chase" bear	$25.00
Charles Woodson #24	$7.00
Charles Woodson #24, white "chase" bear	$14.00
Dan Marino #13	$7.00
Dan Marino #13, white "chase" bear	$22.00
Deion Sanders #21	$7.00
Deion Sanders #21, white "chase" bear	$16.00
Doug Flutie #7	$7.00
Doug Flutie #7, white "chase" bear	$16.00
Drew Bledsoe #11	$7.00
Drew Bledsoe #11, white "chase" bear	$18.00
Jerry Rice #80	$7.00
Jerry Rice #80, white "chase" bear	$18.00
Mark Brunell #8	$7.00
Mark Brunell #8, white "chase" bear	$16.00
Peyton Manning #18	$7.00
Peyton Manning #18, white "chase" bear	$16.00
Randy Moss #84	$7.00
Randy Moss #84, "test"	$15.00
Randy Moss #84, white "chase" bear	$25.00
Terrell Davis #30	$7.00
Terrell Davis #30, white "chase" bear	$18.00

"Premium Pro Bears" Series II (R)

Charlie Batch #10	$7.00
Charlie Batch #10, white "chase" bear	$15.00
Eddie George #27	$7.00
Eddie George #27, white "chase" bear	$15.00
Emmitt Smith #22	$7.00
Emmitt Smith #22, white "chase" bear	$20.00
Jake Plummer #16	$7.00
Jake Plummer #16, white "chase" bear	$16.00
John Elway #7, blue	$7.00
John Elway #7, orange	$10.00
John Elway #7, "test"	$12.00
John Elway #7, white "chase" bear	$25.00
Jamal Anderson #32	$7.00
Jamal Anderson #32, white "chase" bear	$16.00
Keyshawn Johnson #19	$7.00
Keyshawn Johnson #19, white "chase" bear	$16.00
Randall Cunningham #17	$7.00
Randall Cunningham #17, white "chase" bear	$16.00
Ryan Leaf #16	$7.00
Ryan Leaf #16, white "chase" bear	$12.00
Steve Young #8	$7.00
Steve Young #8, "test"	$12.00
Steve Young #8, white "chase" bear	$16.00
Troy Aikman #8	$7.00
Troy Aikman #8, white "chase" bear	$20.00
Vinny Testaverde #16	$7.00
Vinny Testaverde #16, white "chase" bear	$14.00

"Premium Pro Bears" Series III (R)

Carl Pickens #81	$7.00
Chris Carter #80	$7.00
Chris Chandler #12	$7.00
Curtis Martin #28	$7.00
Ed McCaffrey #87	$7.00
Fred Taylor #28	$7.00
Garrison Hearst #20	$7.00
Jerome Bettis #36	$7.00
Joey Galloway #84	$7.00
John Randle #93	$7.00
Junior Seau #55	$7.00
Kordell Stewart #10	$7.00
Marshall Faulk #28	$7.00
Mike Alstott #40	$7.00
Reggie White #92	$7.00
Rich Gannon, #12	$7.00
Robert Edwards #47	$7.00
Shannon Sharpe #84	$7.00
Steve Beuerlein #7	$7.00

Steve McNair #9	$7.00
Terrell Owens #81	$7.00
Terry Glenn #88	$7.00
Tony Boselli #71	$7.00
Warrick Dunn #28	$7.00
Wayne Chrebet #80	$7.00
Zach Thomas #54	$7.00

Denver Broncos Super Bowl Champions

Terrell Davis	$8.00
John Elway (blue tie-dye)	$8.00
John Elway (white, MVP)	$10.00
Ed McCaffrey	$6.00
Bill Romanoski	$6.00
Shannon Sharpe	$6.00

Super Bowl Bear

Super Bowl NFL Players Bear	$20.00

Meanies®

Their name says it all. The Meanies have grown in popularity and collectibility throughout 1998 and 1999. The company's website is at: http://www.meanies.com

Meanies Series 1

Item	S/1999
Series 1	
Armydillo Dan (R)	$5.00
Bart the Elephart (R)	$15.00
Boris the Mucousaurus (R)	$5.00
Fangaroo (Mystery Meanie)	$55.00
Fi & Do the Dalmutation (R)	$5.00
Hurley the Pukin' Toucan (R)	$5.00
Matt the Fat Bat (R)	$6.00
Navy Seal (R)	$15.00
Otis the Octapunk, silver earring (R)	$15.00
Otis the Octapunk, gold earring (R)	$8.00
Peter the Gotta Peegull (R)	$5.00
Sledge the Hammered Head Shark, 6 gills (R)	$25.00
Sledge the Hammered Head Shark, 5 gills (R)	$8.00
Snake Eyes Jake (R)	$9.00
Splat the Road Kill Kat	$5.00
Series 1 1/2	
Lucky the Rabbit (LE 45,000)	$5.00

Series 2

Bare Bear, red mouth	$5.00
Bare Bear, pink mouth	$5.00
Bessie Got Milked!	$5.00
Burny the Bear	$5.00
Chicken Pox	$5.00
Chubby (Mystery Meanie)	$20.00+
Digger the Snottish Terrier	$5.00
Donnie Didn't Duck (R)	$5.00
Floaty the Fish	$5.00
Lucky the Rabbit	$5.00
Peeping Tom Cat, with pupils (R)	$6.00
Pepping Tom Cat, without pupils (R)	$6.00
Phlemingo (R)	$5.00
Sunny the Preemie Chickie	$5.00
Velocicrapper (R)	$7.00

Series 3

Bad Hare Day	$5.00
Dog Eat Dog	$5.00
John Deer	$5.00
No Brainer	$5.00
The Grim Beaver	$5.00
Tied the Bear, white rope	$5.00
Tied the Bear, black rope (LE 10,000)	$5.00
"Si & Mia" the Siamese Cat	$5.00

Meanies Series 3

Infamous Meanies

Bull Clinton, blue tie	$6.00
Bull Clinton, red tie	$6.00
Buddy the Dog, dark chocolate	$6.00
Buddy the Dog, milk chocolate	$6.00
Dennis Rodmantis	$6.00
Donkeyng	$6.00
Jerry Stinger	$6.00
Mallard Stern	$6.00
Mick Jaguar	$6.00
Mike Bison	$6.00
Moodanna	$6.00
Quack Nicholson	$6.00

Limited Edition

Alien Iverson (Philadelphia 76ers, LE 7,500)	$250.00
The Cod Father (Collecting Figures, LE 10,000)	$13.00
Pirate Jack (Madison Scare Garden, LE 10,000)	$250.00

Shocking Stuffer (Holiday 1998)

Splat in the Hat	$5.00
Slushy the Snowman	$5.00
Cold Turkey	$5.00

Valentine's 1999

Got Lucky	$5.00
Heartless Bear, red	$18.00
Heartless Bear, white	$5.00
Stupid Cupid	$5.00

Peaceables®

From Peaceable Planet comes this set of Peaceables, animal bean bags with country or state flags sewn on to show where the animal can be found. The company donates a portion of its profits to charities that support world peace. The first set of eight animal bean bags was released in November 1998; all Peaceables made after Jan. 1, 1999 are numbered, with no more than 72,000 of each character made. Because of a trademark conflict, just 10,000 of the Hue Manatees were made; the name was changed to Mickey Manatee for the next 62,000. These are great bean bags. The company's website is excellent: http://www.peaceableplanet.com

Item	S/1999
Aloha the dolphin (Hawaii)	n/a
Bayou the alligator (Louisiana)	$8.00
Broadway Blue the bluebird (New York)	$8.00
Chimpanzees (special set of 3)	
Clarity (see no evil)	n/a
Frank (speak no evil)	n/a
Harmony (hear no evil)	n/a
C. Sea Lion the sea lion (California)	$8.00
Cool Bleu the polar bear (Canada)	$8.00
Cheech the chihuahua (Mexico)	$8.00
Ho Ping the panda (China)	$8.00
Hue Manatee the manatee (Florida)	$10.00
Lorraine the snail (France)	$8.00
Maximus the elephant (Thailand)	$8.00
Mickey Manatee the manatee (Florida)	$8.00
Myrtle the turtle (South Carolina)	$8.00
Niles the camel (Egypt)	$8.00
Safari the lion (Africa)	$8.00
Savanna the leopard (Kenya)	$8.00
Sherbet O'Shear the sheep (Ireland)	$8.00
Tatonka the buffalo, white face, LE (Montana)	$15.00+
Tatonka the buffalo, red face (Montana)	$8.00
Uncle Sammy the eagle (US)	$8.00

Top: Ho Ping; Middle: Cool Bleu, Uncle Sammy, Cheech, Broadway Blue, Hue Manatee (Mickey Manatee); Bottom: C. Sea Lion, Sherbet O'Shear

Top: Lorraine, Safari, Maximus, Tatonka (white face), Tatonka (red face); Middle: Myrtle, Niles, Savanna; Bottom: Bayou

Precious Moments®

Precious Moments Pals and Precious Moments Tender Tails are licensed by the limited-edition collectibles giant, Enesco. The "Pals" are based on characters from stories in the Precious Moments Videos series. Several of the "Tender Tails" are drawing collector interest. Enesco shares updated information about their Tender Tails on the Internet at: http://www.enesco.com/misc/tndrtail/thome.htm

Item	W/1998	S/1999
Precious Moments Pals		
Alek the lion	n/a	$7.00
Buzz the bee	n/a	$6.00
Dudley the dog, spot over left eye (R)	$7.00	$8.00
Dudley the dog, spots over both eyes (R)	$15.00	$15.00
Georgina the giraffe (R)	$7.00	$16.00
Gill the fish (R)	$100.00	$125.00
Hopper the bird (R)	$7.00	$7.00
Jacob the cat	n/a	$8.00
Jeremy the toucan, green tail (R)	$7.00	$7.00
Jeremy the toucan, orange tail (R)	$15.00	$15.00
Nicodemus the pig	n/a	$8.00
Simon the lamb, blue face (R)	$7.00	$8.00
Simon the lamb, white face (R)	$15.00	$15.00
Snowflake the bunny, white tail (R)	$7.00	$8.00
Snowflake the bunny, pink tail (R)	$15.00	$15.00
Teacher the goose	n/a	$6.00
Thor the dog	n/a	$6.00

Front: Jeremy, Georgina, Dudley;
Back: Simon, Snowflake, Hopper

Item	W/1998	S/1999
Precious Moments Tender Tails		
20th Anniversary Bear, LE 1998 Care-A-Van	$25.00	$15.00
20th Anniversary Panda, LE 1999 Care-A-Van	n/a	$32.00
Bear (R)	$8.00	$9.00
Billy Goat	n/a	$7.00
Blue Bird (R)	$8.00	$8.00
Blue Whale	n/a	$7.00
Brown Bunny	$7.00	$7.00
Brown Cow	n/a	$7.00
Bumblebee	n/a	$7.00
Butterfly	n/a	$7.00
Camel	n/a	$7.00
Canadian Loon, LE, Canada retailers	n/a	$18.00
Canadian Moose, LE, Canada retailers	n/a	$16.00
Cardinal	$7.00	$7.00
Cat	$7.00	$7.00
Chester the pig, LE, fan club MOF	n/a	n/a
Chipmunk	n/a	$7.00
Cow	$7.00	$7.00
Crow	n/a	$7.00
Dark Horse	n/a	$7.00
Donkey	n/a	$7.00
Elephant (R)	$9.00	$12.00
Giraffe, LE, free with gift membership purchase, 1998	$20.00	$125.00
Goose	n/a	$7.00
Gorilla, LE 1999	n/a	$72.00
Green Owl	$7.00	$7.00
Green Whale	n/a	$7.00
Grey Lamb	n/a	$7.00
Harp Seal	$7.00	$7.00
Hippo	$7.00	$7.00
Horse (R)	$8.00	$8.00
Indigo Whale	n/a	$7.00
Koala Bear	n/a	$12.00
Ladybug	n/a	$7.00
Lamb	$7.00	$8.00
Lamb, with W.W.J.D. Bracelet	n/a	$22.00
Lion (R)	$8.00	$8.00
Monkey	$7.00	$7.00
Orange Whale	n/a	$7.00
Palm Tree	n/a	$7.00
Parrot, LE 1999	n/a	n/a
Peach Pig	n/a	$7.00
Penguin	$7.00	$7.00
Pink Bunny	$7.00	$7.00
Pink Flamingo, LE 1999	n/a	$11.00
Pink Pig (R)	$8.00	$9.00
Polar Bear	$7.00	$7.00

Front: Elephant, Bear, Turtle; Back: Lion, Pink Pig, Horse

Front: Brown Bunny, Pink Bunny, White Bunny; Back: Yellow Duck, Blue Bird, Lamb

White Rhino

Red Whale	n/a	$7.00
Reindeer	$7.00	$7.00
Rooster	n/a	$7.00
Rosie the mouth, LE, free with purchase of select PM figurine	n/a	$10.00
Skunk	n/a	$7.00
Snowman	$15.00	$15.00
Spider Monkey, gray, PM figurine premium	n/a	$10.00
Spider Monkey, light brown, PM figurine premium	n/a	$10.00
Spider Monkey, dark brown, PM figurine premium	n/a	$10.00
Squirrel	n/a	$7.00
Tippy (R)	n/a	$8.00
Toucan, LE, free with gift membership purchase 1999	n/a	$40.00
Turkey	n/a	$7.00
Turkey with Sign	n/a	$7.00
Turtle (R)	$9.00	$15.00
Tyedye Whale	n/a	$7.00
Unicorn, LE 1998	$10.00	$15.00
Violet Whale	n/a	$7.00
White and Lavender Bunny	n/a	$7.00
White Bunny	$7.00	$7.00
White Duck	n/a	$7.00
White Owl, LE, PM figurine premium	$10.00	$12.00
White Rhino, LE 1998	$15.00	$14.00
Yellow Duck (R)	$8.00	$8.00
Yellow Whale	n/a	$7.00

Top: Elephant, Bear, Horse; Bottom: Lion, Turtle, Pink Pig

Top: Snowman, Reindeer; Bottom: Polar Bear, Harp Seal

Top: Cow, Monkey, Green Owl; Bottom: Hippo, Cat, Blue Bird

Tender Tails "Certificate of Adoption"

Puffkins®

Puffkins have caught on among collectors. The hard-to-find Puffkins, such as Lily, Shelly, and Snowball variations, garner high values. Puffkins has a great website offering lots of collector information at: http://www.swibco.com

Item	W/1998	S/1999
Albert the alligator	n/a	$6.00
Amber the monkey	$7.00	$6.00
Armour the armadillo (R)	$20.00	$35.00
Aussie the koala	$7.00	$6.00
Baldwin the eagle	$7.00	$6.00
Bandit the raccoon	$7.00	$6.00
Benny the bear	$7.00	$8.00
Biff the buffalo	$7.00	$6.00
Bluebelle the lamb	n/a	$6.00
Bosley the bulldog	n/a	$6.00
Bruno the bull	n/a	$6.00
Bumper the rabbit	n/a	$6.00
Buttercup the bear	n/a	$6.00
Casey the cardinal	$7.00	$6.00
Chirps the chick	n/a	$6.00
Chomper the beaver	$7.00	$6.00
Cinder the dalmatian (R)	$7.00	$7.00
Cinnamon the cat	$7.00	$6.00
Crystal the bear	n/a	$6.00
Danny the purple dinosaur	n/a	$7.00
Ding the bat	$9.00	$7.00
Dinky the dinosaur (R)	$15.00	$10.00
Dottie the ladybug	n/a	$6.00
Drake the dinosaur (R)	$15.00	$10.00
Elly the elephant (R)	$7.00	$7.00
Fetch the dog, dark nose (R)	n/a	$7.00
Fetch the dog, light nose (R)	n/a	$10.00
Flo the flamingo	n/a	$6.00
Flurry the snowman	$9.00	$6.00
Franklin the fox	n/a	$6.00
Freddy the tree frog	n/a	$7.00
Ginger the giraffe	$7.00	$6.00
Gourdy the pumpkin	$9.00	$10.00
Grizwald the bear	n/a	$6.00
Gus the moose	$7.00	$6.00
Happy the smiley face	n/a	$6.00
Hazel the witch	$9.00	$11.00
Henrietta the hippo	$7.00	$6.00
Ho Ho the Santa	$9.00	$6.00
Honey the bear (R)	$7.00	$7.00
Hugs the bear	n/a	$6.00
Jingles the bear	$9.00	$7.00
Kisses the bear	n/a	$6.00
Lancaster the lion	$7.00	$6.00
Lenny the leopard	n/a	$6.00
Lily the frog, 2-29-97, bright green feet	$40.00	$50.00

Top: Tibbs, Odie, Zack; Middle: Lizzy, Ginger, Shadow; Bottom: Toby, Peeps

Top: Henrietta, Max, Lucky; 2nd Row: Lily, Peter, Amber; 3rd Row: Percy, Trixy, Bandit; Bottom: Milo, Murphy

150

Lily the frog, 2-28-97, dark green feet	$7.00	$7.00
Lizzy the lamb	$7.00	$6.00
Lucky the rabbit	$7.00	$6.00
Mango the bear	n/a	$6.00
Max the gorilla (R)	$7.00	$7.00
Meadow the cow	$7.00	$6.00
Milo the monkey	$7.00	$6.00
Murphy the mouse	$7.00	$6.00
Nutty the squirrel	$7.00	$6.00
Odie the skunk	$7.00	$6.00
Olley the owl	$7.00	$6.00
Omar the orangutan	n/a	$6.00
Patrick the bear	n/a	$6.00
Patriot the eagle	n/a	$7.00
Patty the bear	n/a	$6.00
Paws the cat	$7.00	$6.00
Peeps the chick	$7.00	$6.00
Percy the pig	$7.00	$6.00
Peter the panda	$7.00	$6.00
Pickles the dinosaur (R)	$15.00	$10.00
Quakster the duck	$7.00	$6.00
Red the devil	$9.00	$8.00
Rosie the bear	n/a	$10.00
Scooter the chipmunk	n/a	$6.00
Shadow the cat (R)	$7.00	$12.00
Shaggs the sheep dog	n/a	$6.00
Shelly the turtle, bright green feet (R)	$40.00	$35.00
Shelly the turtle, dark green feet (R)	$7.00	$7.00
Skylar the bear	n/a	$6.00
Slick the seal	$7.00	$6.00
Snowball the tiger, black nose (R)	$150.00	$175.00
Snowball the tiger, pink nose (R)	$40.00	$45.00
Snowball the tiger, lavender nose (R)	$40.00	$50.00
Spike the porcupine	n/a	$6.00
Squawk the parrot	n/a	$6.00
Strut the turkey	n/a	$6.00
Swoop the falcon	n/a	$6.00
Tasha the tiger, light pink nose	$12.00	$9.00
Tasha the tiger, pink nose	$7.00	$6.00
Telly the bear	n/a	$6.00
Tibbs the rabbit	$7.00	$6.00
Tiki the toucan	$7.00	$6.00
Tipper the tiger, green eyes	$12.00	$12.00
Tipper the tiger, yellow eyes	$7.00	$6.00
Toby the whale (R)	$7.00	$7.00
Trixy the monkey	$7.00	$6.00
Tux the penguin	$7.00	$6.00
Violet the bear	n/a	$6.00
Whiskers the walrus	n/a	$6.00
Zack the zebra	$7.00	$6.00

Top: Benny, Olley, Quakster; 2nd Row: Tipper, Cinder, Honey; 3rd Row: Biff, Fetch, Bandit; Bottom: Aussie, Snowball (pink nose

Top: Elly, Lancaster, Meadow; 2nd Row: Tux, Chomper, Nutty; 3rd Row: Gus, Paws, Shelly (dark green feet); Bottom: Slick

Russ Bean Bags®

Russ Berrie & Company, Inc., a leading maker of gifts, teddy bears, and a wide range of other merchandise, has issued two darling sets of bean bags. Home Buddies are sweet and country-ish in design, made of stonewashed natural cotton, each with its own birthdate. The Wishlings are cool-looking, made of a shiny cloth material. Each has its own birthdate, as well. Both lines of bean bags are of very high quality and are enjoyed by many collectors.

Item	W/1998	S/1999
Russ Home Buddies Bean Bags		
Biff the cow	$8.00	$8.00
Bubbles the hippo	$8.00	$8.00
Cashew the elephant	$8.00	$8.00
Cheezy the mouse	$8.00	$8.00
Chobee the dinosaur	$8.00	$8.00
Coco the monkey	$8.00	$8.00
Cozy the dog	$8.00	$8.00
Crackers the lobster	$8.00	$8.00
Hamlet the pig	$8.00	$8.00
L'il Gator the alligator	$8.00	$8.00
Nibbles the bunny	$8.00	$8.00
Perky the penguin	$8.00	$8.00
Punchy the panda	$8.00	$8.00
Ribbity the frog	$8.00	$8.00
Ringo the dog	$8.00	$8.00
Romper the dog	$8.00	$8.00
Sly the bear	$8.00	$8.00
Sniffy the mouse	$8.00	$8.00
Stilts the flamingo	$8.00	$8.00
Zippy the zebra	$8.00	$8.00
Zulu the lion	$8.00	$8.00
Russ Wishlings Bean Bags		
Cappuccino the dog	$10.00	$10.00
Mocha the monkey	$10.00	$10.00
Pasha the gold dog	$10.00	$10.00
Pasha the gray dog	$10.00	$10.00
Peanut the gray elephant	$10.00	$10.00
Peanut the pink elephant	$10.00	$10.00
Pickles the pig	$10.00	$10.00
Pistachio the frog	$10.00	$10.00
Praline the lion	$10.00	$10.00
Puckers the blue and purple fish	$10.00	$10.00
Puckers the pink and green fish	$10.00	$10.00
Punch the panda	$10.00	$10.00
Rollo the rhinoceros	$10.00	$10.00
Tasha the cat	$10.00	$10.00
Truffles the bear	$10.00	$10.00
Warts the frog	$10.00	$10.00

Salvino's Bammers®

Salvino's Bammers is a great line of officially licensed, limited-edition bears (plus a bee, butterfly, and bunnies). They are the only bean bag products allowed to use the names and numbers of Major League Baseball players! Because of the popularity of Bammers, the company has branched out into other sports and the entertainment world, as well. Bammers are great additions to any collection. For information on the Internet about Salvino's Bammers go to: http://www.bammers.com

Item	W/1998	S/1999
Promo Bammers		
Muhammad Ali, bear	n/a	$45.00
John Elway (orange/blue)	n/a	$45.00
Wayne Gretzky (full-size, blue/gold)	n/a	$50.00
Wayne Gretzky (Baby Bammer-size, blue/gold)	n/a	$25.00
Mark McGwire (red)	$300.00	$175.00
Sammy Sosa (blue tie-dye)	n/a	$45.00
Baseball Bammers		
1998 Commemorative Gold Set (R)		
Dante Bichette (purple)	$30.00	$35.00
Juan Gonzalez (red)	$38.00	$23.00
Ken Griffey Jr. (green)	$60.00	$25.00
Tony Gwynn (creamy gold)	$35.00	$40.00
Derek Jeter (white)	$42.00	$35.00
Greg Maddux (gray)	$35.00	$24.00
Mark McGwire (red)	$150.00	$60.00
Mike Piazza (white)	$45.00	$38.00
Cal Ripken Jr (orange)	$50.00	$34.00
Gary Sheffield (blue)	$30.00	$22.00
Frank Thomas (white)	$35.00	$30.00
Kerry Wood (blue)	$40.00	$18.00
1998 Rocky's All Star Set (Colorado) (R)		
Dante Bichette (purple)	$60.00	$50.00
Vinny Castilla (purple)	$75.00	$65.00
Larry Walker (purple)	$75.00	$65.00
1998 Summer Edition (R)		
Barry Bonds (orange)	$12.00	$8.00
Roger Clemens (blue)	$13.00	$8.00
Jim Edmonds (white)	$13.00	$7.00
Ken Griffey Jr. (tie-dye)	$17.00	$8.00
Chipper Jones (lavender)	$15.00	$7.00
David Justice (maroon)	$12.00	$7.00
Tino Martinez (gold)	$11.00	$7.00
Mark McGwire (purple)	$35.00	$8.00
Cal Ripken Jr. (dark blue)	$16.00	$8.00
Alex Rodriguez (tie-dye)	$12.00	$7.00
Ivan Rodriguez (cream)	$12.00	$7.00
Sammy Sosa (red)	$18.00	$9.00

Item	S/1999
1998 Holiday Set (R)	
Ken Griffey Jr.	$8.00
Chipper Jones	$7.00
Dave Justice	$7.00
Mark McGwire	$8.00
Cal Ripken Jr.	$8.00
Alex Rodriguez	$7.00

1998 Holiday Set

1998 Roberto Clemente (R)

Roberto Clemente
(gold with Puerto
Rico flag) — $25.00

Roberto
Clemente

1998 Home
Rung Kings
Set

1998 Home Run Kings Set	
Roger Maris	$6.00
Mark McGwire	$7.00
Babe Ruth	$7.00
Sammy Sosa	$7.00

1998 New York Yankees World Series Set	
Scott Brosius	$6.00
Orlando Hernandez	$6.00
Derek Jeter	$7.00
Tino Martinez	$6.00
Darryl Strawberry	$6.00
David Wells	$6.00

1998 New York
Yankees World
Series Set

1998 Award Winners Set	
Roger Clemens	$6.00
Tom Glavine	$6.00
Juan Gonzalez	$6.00
Ben Grieve	$6.00
Ken Griffey Jr.	$7.00
Mark McGwire	$10.00
Sammy Sosa	$8.00
Kerry Wood	$6.00

1998 Award Winners Set

1999 Opening Day Baseball	
Jeff Bagwell (white/gold stars)	$7.00
Albert Belle (orange/black)	$6.00
Roger Clemens (black/white)	$6.00
J.D. Drew (red/white)	$6.00
Nomar Garciaparra (red/blue)	$6.00
Derek Jeter (white/ black pinstripes)	$7.00
Randy Johnson (green/purple)	$6.00
Mark McGwire (red/white)	$8.00
Mike Piazza (blue/red)	$7.00
Sammy Sosa (blue/red, white and blue)	$7.00
Mo Vaughn (blue/gold)	$6.00
David Wells (black/white)	$6.00
Kerry Wood (red/white/blue)	$6.00

1999 Opening Day
Baseball—Top: Jeter,
Garciaparra, Sosa,
Drew; Middle: Vaughn,
McGwire, Piazza,
Bagwell, Wood,
Johnson; Bottom:
Clemens, Belle

1999 Fourth of July Set

Ken Griffey Jr.	n/a
Derek Jeter	n/a
Mark McGwire	n/a
Mike Piazza	n/a
Cal Ripken Jr.	n/a
Sammy Sosa	n/a

1999 Bamm Bunnies

J.D. Drew	$6.00
Ken Griffey Jr.	$7.00
Derek Jeter	$6.00
Chipper Jones	$6.00
Mark McGwire	$8.00
Sammy Sosa	$7.00

1999 Bamm Bunnies—
Top: Jones, Griffey,
McGwire; Bottom: Jeter,
Sosa, Drew

1999 Baby Bammers

Mark McGwire and J.D. Drew	n/a
Dante Bichette and Larry Walker	n/a
Kevin Brown and Gary Sheffield	n/a
Tony Gwynn and Wally Joyner	n/a
Jeff Bagwell and Ken Caminiti	n/a
Sammy Sosa and Mark Grace	n/a
Mike Piazza and Robin Ventura	n/a
Derek Jeter and Roger Clemens	n/a
Derek Jeter and David Wells	n/a
Cal Ripken Jr. and Will Clark	n/a
Nomar Garciaparra and John Valentin	n/a
Roberto Alomar and Sandy Alomar	n/a
Tim Salmon and Darin Erstad	n/a
Juan Gonzalez and Rusty Greer	n/a
Wade Boggs and Jose Canseco	n/a
Ken Griffey Jr. and Edgar Martinez	n/a
Jason Giambi and Ben Grieve	n/a

Baby Bammers prototypes

Mark McGwire (red/white, coarse fabric, no tush-tag)	n/a
Mark McGwire (red/white, plush fabric, no hang-tag)	n/a
Sammy Sosa (blue/white, coarse fabric, no tush-tag)	n/a
Sammy Sosa (blue/white, plush fabric, no hang-tag)	n/a

The coarse-fabric Bammers are found with or without hang-tags. Sosa most commonly has a Dante Bichette tag; the McGwire has Mark McGwire Commemorative Gold tag.

1999 International Set

Juan Gonzalez (Puerto Rico)	n/a
Chan Ho Park (Korea)	n/a
Andruw Jones (Curacao)	n/a
Mark McGwire (U.S.)	n/a
Sammy Sosa (Dominican Republic)	n/a
Larry Walker (Canada)	n/a

1999 Ballpark Bammers I

(These Bammers were sold at the home ballparks of each ballplayer.)

Roberto Alomar (Cleveland Indians)	n/a
Kevin Brown (Los Angeles Dodgers)	n/a
Mike Caruso (Chicago White Sox)	n/a
Eric Chavez (Oakland Athletics)	n/a

Item	S/1999
Andres Galarraga (Atlanta Braves)	n/a
Jason Giambi (Oakland Athletics)	n/a
Tom Glavine (Atlanta Braves)	n/a
Juan Gonzalez (Texas Rangers)	n/a
Ben Grieve (Oakland Athletics)	n/a
Todd Hundley (Los Angeles Dodgers)	n/a
Randy Johnson (Arizona Diamondbacks)	n/a
Chipper Jones (Atlanta Braves)	n/a
Eric Karros (Los Angeles Dodgers)	n/a
Travis Lee (Arizona Diamondbacks)	n/a
Kenny Lofton (Cleveland Indians)	n/a
Javy Lopez (Atlanta Braves)	n/a
Greg Maddux (Atlanta Braves)	n/a
Raul Mondesi (Los Angeles Dodgers)	n/a
Ivan Rodriguez (Texas Rangers)	n/a
Scott Rolen (Philadelphia Phillies)	n/a
Gary Sheffield (Los Angeles Dodgers)	n/a
Matt Stairs (Oakland Athletics)	n/a
Frank Thomas (Chicago White Sox)	n/a
Jim Thome (Cleveland Indians)	n/a
Omar Vizquel (Cleveland Indians)	n/a
Devon White (Los Angeles Dodgers)	n/a
Matt Williams (Arizona Diamondbacks)	n/a

1999 All-Star Game

Nomar Garciaparra (Boston Red Sox)	n/a
Pedro Martinez (Boston Red Sox)	n/a
Tom Gordon (Boston Red Sox)	$7.00

Sports-Event Giveaways

Henry Aaron, LA Dodgers, 4/8/99 (27,000)	$28.00
Michael Barrett, Harrisburg Senators, 6/18/99	n/a
Duke, Albuquerque Dukes, 6/27/99	n/a
Jim Edmonds, California Angela, 5/1/99 (10,000)	n/a
Alex Fernandez, Florida Marlins, 5/1/99 (20,000)	n/a
Cliff Floyd, Harrisburg Senators	n/a
Ken Griffey Jr., LA Dodgers, 4/11/99 (27,000)	$45.00
Vladimir Guerrero, Harrisburg Senators, 5/2/99	n/a
Derek Jeter, Columbus Clippers, 7/4/99	n/a
Bobby "Jonesy" Jones, Tulsa Drillers, 5/2/99	n/a
Paul Kariya, Mighty Ducks, 1/10/99 (3,500)	$45.00
Roger Maris, LA Dodgers, 4/10/99 (27,000)	$20.00
Mark McGwire, Columbus Clippers, 4/16/99	n/a
Mark McGwire, LA Dodgers, 4/6/99 (27,000)	$45.00
Mark McGwire, Reading Phillies, 6/18/99	n/a

Item	S/1999
Scott Rolen, Philadelphia Phillies, 5/17/99 (17,000)	n/a
Scott Rolen, Reading Phillies, 7/11/99	n/a
Babe Ruth, LA Dodgers, 4/7/99 (27,000)	$25.00
Nolan Ryan, SSPC	n/a
Nolan Ryan, Texas Rangers	n/a
Tim Salmon, California Angels, 9/18/99 (10,000)	n/a
Curt Schilling, Reading Phillies, 7/26/99	n/a
Teemu Selanne, Mighty Ducks, 1/10/99 (3,500)	$45.00
Sammy Sosa, Columbus Clippers, 4/16/99	n/a
Sammy Sosa, LA Dodgers, 4/9/99 (27,000)	$25.00
Sammy Sosa, Reading Phillies, 8/10/99	n/a
Mo Vaughn, California Angels, 5/15/99 (10,000)	n/a
Bernie Williams, Columbus Clippers, 5/31/99	n/a

1999 Salvino's Bammers Collector's Club
Mark McGwire, furry (brown/red)	n/a

1999 Team Best Set
Ryan Anderson (Wisconsin Timber Rattlers)	n/a
Rick Ankiel (Peoria Chiefs)	n/a
Lance Berkman (New Orleans Zephyrs)	n/a
Pat Burrell (Clearwater Phillies)	n/a
J.D. Drew (Memphis Redbirds)	n/a
J.D. Drew (Arkansas Travelers)	n/a

1999 Signature Series
Item	S/1999
Henry Aaron (715)	$140.00
Nancy Kerrigan	n/a
Tara Lipinski	n/a
Joe Montana (1,979) (R)	$110.00
Joe Namath (1,969) (R)	$100.00
Joe Namath, Alabama	n/a

Joe Namath
Signature Series
Bammer

Football Bammers
1999 Football Series I (R)
Troy Aikman	$12.00
Drew Bledsoe	$7.00
Brett Favre	$10.00
Terrell Davis (blue)	$8.00
Terrell Davis (orange)	$7.00
John Elway (blue)	$12.00
John Elway (orange)	$10.00
Ryan Leaf	$7.00
Peyton Manning	$7.00
Item	**S/1999**

Dan Marino	$9.00
Jerry Rice	$7.00
Kordell Stewart	$7.00
Vinny Testaverde	$7.00
Steve Young	$7.00

1999 Super Bowl Set

Terry Bradshaw	$8.00
Brett Favre	$8.00
John Elway	$10.00
Joe Montana (San Francisco 49ers)	$10.00
Joe Namath (New York Jets)	$8.00
Steve Young	$8.00

Top: Marino, Manning; Middle: Leaf, Favre, Aikman, Young, Elway, Davis, Rice; Bottom: Bledsoe, Stewart, Testaverde

1999 John Elway Prototype

| John Elway (orange/blue, diamond-shaped hang-tag, no emblem, no "Promo" on sleeves) | n/a |

Hockey Bammers

1999 Hockey Bammers

Sergei Fedorov	$8.00
Peter Forsberg	$7.00
Wayne Gretzky	$10.00
Dominik Hasek	$7.00
Brett Hull	$7.00
Jaromir Jagr	$8.00
Paul Kariya	$7.00
Eric Lindros	$8.00
Mark Messier	$7.00
Patrick Roy	$7.00
Brendan Shanahan	$10.00
Steve Yzerman	$10.00

1999 Wayne Gretzky Set

Wayne Gretzky (black/silver)	$9.00
Wayne Gretzky (blue/red)	$9.00
Wayne Gretzky (orange/blue)	$9.00
Wayne Gretzky (red/white/ maple leaf), Canada exclusive	$35.00

1999 Figure Skating

Scott Hamilton	n/a
Dorothy Hamill	n/a
Nancy Kerrigan	n/a
Tara Lipinski	n/a
Elvis Stojko	n/a
Katerina Witt	n/a

1999 Country Stars

Alan Jackson	n/a
Tim McCoy	n/a
Faith Hill	n/a
Item	**S/1999**

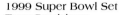

Reba McIntire	n/a	
LeAnn Rimes	n/a	
Randy Travis	n/a	
Travis Tritt	n/a	
Shania Twain	n/a	

1999 Muhammad Ali Set

Muhammad Ali, bee	$7.00
Muhammad Ali, bear	$7.00
Muhammad Ali, bear (Wheaties offer)	$40.00
Muhammad Ali, butterfly	$7.00

Save the Children Bean Bag Plush®

These are interesting and unique sets of bean bags. They are from the Save the Children Foundation, and 5% of the retail price is donated to the foundation. They are pricey at $8, but they are very well made, especially their clothing.

Item	W/1998	S/1999
1998 Collection		
Haruko	$8.00	$8.00
Juji	$8.00	$8.00
Mackenzie	$8.00	$8.00
Patrick	$8.00	$8.00
Paz	$8.00	$8.00
Sila	$8.00	$8.00
1999 Collection		
Damita	n/a	$8.00
Erik	n/a	$8.00
Kachina	n/a	$8.00
Jun	n/a	$8.00
Stella	n/a	$8.00
Stephane	n/a	$8.00

Front: Patrick, Paz, Silz; Back: Haruko, Juji, Mackenzie

Star Beans®

Mattel has premiered a new set of bean bags—Star Beans! They are the only bean bags that come with a plastic protector safeguarding the collectible tag. Featuring a signature star streamer attachment in bright yellow, this unique accessory securely fastens the plastic protector and hang-tag to the Star Bean. Additionally, each hang-tag offers neat and interesting facts about each character. Mattel has said that it will have retirement and new character announcements. A website is under construction, as well, at: http://www.star-beans.com The 101 Dalmatians set was available exclusively through an offer on the Disney 101 Dalmatians video. The Star Beans are available at mass retail outlets $4.99.

Item	S/1999
101 Dalmatians	
Freckles	$8.00
Patch	$8.00
Penny	$8.00
Pepper	$8.00
Disney Classics Series	
Baloo	$5.00
Bambi	$5.00
Dumbo	$5.00
King Louie	$5.00
Thumper	$5.00
Timothy	$5.00
Mickey Mouse Series	
Chip	$5.00
Daisy Duck	$5.00
Dale	$5.00
Donald Duck	$5.00
Goofy	$5.00
Mickey Mouse	$5.00
Minnie Mouse	$5.00
Pluto	$5.00
Winnie-the-Pooh Series	
Eeyore	$5.00
Gopher	$5.00
Kanga & Roo	$5.00
Owl	$5.00
Piglet	$5.00
Rabbit	$5.00
Tigger	$5.00
Winnie-the-Pooh	$5.00

Star Beans Tag

Top: Gopher, Piglet, Tigger, Kanga & Roo, Owl, Goofy; 2nd Row: Rabbit, Winnie-the-Pooh, Eeyore, Minnie Mouse, Pluto; 3rd Row: Rabbit, Bambi, Dumbo, Mickey Mouse, Chip; Bottom: King Louie, Baloo, Timothy, Daisy Duck, Donald Duck, Dale

Star Sacks Celebrity Bean Bags®

These unique bean bags are part of "White's Guide Exclusives" series.

Chipper Jones 1E, Dennis Rodman
(green, red, yellow hair), and Reggie White

Item	W/1998	S/1999
Buffalo Bill	n/a	$15.00
Al Scarface Capone	n/a	$15.00
Bill Clinton	n/a	$15.00
Hillary Clinton	n/a	$15.00
General Custer	n/a	$15.00
James Dean	n/a	$15.00
Chipper Jones, black eye (1E 6,000)	$15.00	$15.00
Chipper Jones, no black eye (2E)	n/a	$15.00
Robert E. Lee	n/a	$15.00
Dennis Rodman, special edition AIDS logo	n/a	$20.00
Dennis Rodman, green hair (1E 8,500)	$15.00	$15.00
Dennis Rodman, red hair (1E 8,500)	$15.00	$15.00
Dennis Rodman, tie-dyed hair (2E)	n/a	$15.00
Dennis Rodman, yellow hair (1E 8,500)	$15.00	$15.00
Babe Ruth	n/a	$15.00
Kordell Stewart	n/a	$15.00
Reggie White (1E 6,000)	$15.00	$15.00

The Velveteen Bean Bear Company®

Three of the finest bean bags you'll ever see are from England, courtesy of The Velveteen Bean Bear Company (TVBBC). These beautiful bears were designed by Tina Watson. They are not often found for sale.

Item	S/1999
Beefeater bear	$20.00
British Bobby bear	$20.00
Buckingham Palace bear	$20.00

Bears—Buckingham
Palace, Beefeater,
British Bobby

Sports
Related

Anaheim Angels Mascots®

With Disney purchasing the former California Angels
baseball team came a change in name (to Anaheim
Angles) and the introduction of a set of very high-quality
bean bags. These were ordered through the Angels
Internet site: http://www.angelsbaseball.com

Clutch and Scoop

Item	W/1998	S/1999
Clutch	$16.00	$13.00
Scoop	$12.00	$10.00

Australian Football League

From my source "down under," I found out about these
Australian Football League (Australian Rules Football) bears.
Each of these bean bags is really the same bear, only wear-
ing the shirt of its respective team.

Item	S/1999
Adelaide Crows	$8.00
Brisbane Lions	$8.00
Carlton Blues	$8.00
Collingwood Magpies	$8.00
Essendon Bombers	$8.00
Fremantle Dockers	$8.00
Geelong Cats	$8.00
Hawthorn Hawks	$8.00
Melbourne Demons	$8.00
North Melbourne Kangaroos	$8.00
Port Adelaide	$8.00
Richmond Tigers	$8.00
St. Kilda Saints	$8.00
Sydney Swans	$8.00
West Coast Eagles	$8.00
Western Bulldogs	$8.00

St. Kilda Saints

College Mascots®

As you can see by the number of new listings, there have been numerous college mascot bean bags added to the set over the past year. They are popular within the regions of the schools.

University of Colorado "Ralphie"

Brutus Buckeye

Item	W/1998	S/1999
Arizona State, Sparky	n/a	$8.00
Auburn, Tiger	$8.00	$8.00
Baylor, Bear	n/a	$8.00
Clemson, Tiger	$8.00	$8.00
Colorado State, Ram	n/a	$8.00
Drake, Bulldog	n/a	$8.00
Duke, Blue Devil	n/a	$8.00
East Carolina	n/a	$8.00
Florida, Alligator	$8.00	$8.00
Florida State, Horse	n/a	$10.00
Fresno State, Bulldog	n/a	$8.00
Georgetown, Bulldog	n/a	$8.00
Georgia, Bulldog	$8.00	$8.00
Georgia Tech, Buzz	n/a	$9.00
Iowa State, Cardinal	$8.00	$8.00
Kansas State, Wildcat	$8.00	$8.00
Louisiana State, Tiger	$8.00	$8.00
Louisville, Cardinal	$8.00	$8.00
Marshall, Buffalo	n/a	$8.00
Miami of Ohio, Red Bird	n/a	$8.00
Mississippi State, Bulldog	n/a	$8.00
Mississippi State, Bulldog, Shoney's Restaurant	n/a	$10.00
Missouri, Tiger	n/a	$8.00
Montana, Grizzly Bear	n/a	$8.00
North Carolina State, Wolf	n/a	$8.00
Northern Iowa, Bear	n/a	$8.00
Northwestern, Wildcat	n/a	$8.00
Notre Dame, Fighting Irishman	n/a	$8.00
Ohio State, Buckeye	n/a	$8.00
Ohio State, Brutus Buckeye (McDonald's)	n/a	$14.00
Ohio State, Band Member	n/a	$10.00
Ohio University, Bobcat	n/a	$8.00

Oklahoma State, Cowpoke	n/a	$8.00
Oregon State, Beaver	n/a	$8.00
Penn State, Lion	$8.00	$8.00
Penn State, Lion with Santa hat	n/a	$8.00
Pittsburgh, Bear	n/a	$8.00
Purdue, Bear	n/a	$8.00
Purdue, Purdue Pete Beany (Burger King, LE 20,000)	n/a	$20.00
Purdue, Purdue Pete Beany II (Burger King, LE 20,000)	n/a	$12.00
Texas A&M, Dog	n/a	$8.00
Texas Tech, Man	n/a	$8.00
UCLA, "Joe" Bruin	n/a	$8.00
U of Alabama, Elephant	$8.00	$8.00
U of Arizona, Wildcat	$8.00	$8.00
U of Arkansas, Razorback	n/a	$8.00
U of Colorado, Buffalo "Ralphie"	$8.00	$8.00
U of Connecticut, Husky	n/a	$8.00
U of Iowa, Hawkeye	$8.00	$8.00
U of Kansas, Jayhawk	$8.00	$8.00
U of Kentucky, Wildcat	$8.00	$8.00
U of Kentucky, Wildcat, NCAA Championship	$10.00	$12.00
U of Maryland, Terrapin	n/a	$8.00
U of Miami, Ibis	n/a	$8.00
U of Michigan, Wolverine	n/a	$8.00
U of Minnesota, Gopher	n/a	$8.00
U of Mississippi, Colonel Reb	n/a	$8.00
U of Nebraska, baseball "Lil Red"	$8.00	$8.00
U of Nebraska, football "Herbie"	$8.00	$8.00
U of New Mexico, Fox	n/a	$8.00
U of North Carolina, Goat	$8.00	$8.00
U of Oklahoma, Dog	n/a	$8.00
U of Rhode Island, Ram	n/a	$8.00
U of South Carolina, Gamecock	n/a	$8.00
U of Tennessee, Dog	$8.00	$8.00
U of Texas, Longhorn	n/a	$8.00
U of Washington, Wildcat	n/a	$8.00
U of Wisconsin, Badger	$8.00	$8.00
U.S. Naval Academy, Bear	n/a	$8.00
Washington State, Cougar	n/a	$8.00
West Texas, Bear	n/a	$8.00
West Texas A&M, Buffalo	n/a	$8.00
West Virginia, Mountaineer	n/a	$8.00
Western Kentucky	n/a	$8.00
Wyoming, Cowboy	n/a	$8.00

ESPN® Bean Bags

These bean bags were sold at "ESPN The Store," located in Disney World. They are generic sports characters with no player or team affiliations. (Note: Disney owns ESPN.)

Baseball Player M/W, Extrovert green, Extrovert gold, Basketball player M/B

Item	W/1998	S/1999
Baseball player, male/black	$10.00	$14.00
Baseball player, male/white	$10.00	$10.00
Basketball player, male/black	$12.00	$8.00
Basketball player, male/white	$12.00	$14.00
Extrovert (X-Games mascot), dark green/orange	$18.00	$15.00
Extrovert (X-Games mascot), gold/white	$12.00	$15.00
Extrovert (X-Games mascot), light green/dark green	$20.00	$15.00
Extrovert (X-Games mascot), orange/light green	$14.00	$15.00
Extrovert (X-Games mascot), white/dark green	$22.00	$15.00
Football player, male/black	$10.00	$10.00
Football player, male/white	$13.00	$10.00
Golfer, female/white	$9.00	$8.00
Golfer, male/black	$8.00	$11.00
Golfer, male/white	$8.00	$10.00
Hockey player	$25.00	$45.00
Referee	$15.00	$20.00
Soccer player, female/white	$14.00	$15.00
Soccer player, male/black	$9.00	$15.00
Soccer player, male/white	$10.00	$15.00
Tennis player, female/white	$12.00	$22.00
Tennis player, male/white	$8.00	$8.00

Fanimals®

Bean bag bears made for professional baseball, basketball, football, and hockey teams.

Item	S/1999
Baseball	
Anaheim Angels	$7.00
Arizona Diamondbacks	$7.00
Atlanta Braves	$7.00
Baltimore Orioles	$7.00
Boston Red Sox	$7.00
Chicago Cubs	$7.00
Chicago White Sox	$7.00
Cincinnati Reds	$7.00
Cleveland Indians	$7.00
Colorado Rockies	$7.00

Florida Marlins	$7.00
Los Angeles Dodgers	$7.00
New York Yankees	$7.00
Oakland A's	$7.00
Pittsburgh Pirates	$7.00
St. Louis Cardinals	$7.00
Seattle Mariners	$7.00
Tampa Bay Devil Rays	$7.00
Texas Rangers	$7.00

Basketball
Boston Celtics	$7.00
Charlotte Hornets	$7.00
Chicago Bulls	$7.00
Houston Rockets	$7.00
Los Angeles Lakers	$7.00
Miami Heat	$7.00
New York Knicks	$7.00
Orlando Magic	$7.00
Phoenix Suns	$7.00
San Antonio Spurs	$7.00
Utah Jazz	$7.00

Football
Atlanta Falcons	$7.00
Carolina Panthers	$7.00
Chicago Bears	$7.00
Dallas Cowboys	$7.00
Denver Broncos	$7.00
Green Bay Packers	$7.00
Jacksonville Jaguars	$7.00
Kansas City Chiefs	$7.00
Miami Dolphins	$7.00
New England Patriots	$7.00
New York Giants	$7.00
New York Jets	$7.00
Pittsburgh Steelers	$7.00
San Francisco 49'ers	$7.00
Tampa Bay Buccaneers	$7.00

Green Bay Packers
Bear

Hockey
Anaheim Mighty Ducks	$7.00
Carolina Hurricanes	$7.00
Chicago Blackhawks	$7.00
Detroit Redwings	$7.00
New Jersey Devils	$7.00
New York Rangers	$7.00
Philadelphia Flyers	$7.00
Pittsburgh Penguins	$7.00
Tampa Bay Lightning	$7.00

Footix®

Bird mascot for the 1998 World Cup Soccer tournament held in France. An excellent foreign-issued bean bag.

Item	S/1999
Footix	$12.00

L.A. Dodgers Beanpals®

A pair of limited edition Beanpals were made for the Los Angeles Dodgers.

Item	W/1998	S/1999
Bearbino Bear	$18.00	$15.00
Li'l Blue Dog	n/a	$8.00

Bearbino

Mighty Ducks Wild Wing®

The Anaheim Mighty Ducks hockey team mascot was made into a couple of bean bags. The Mighty Ducks is a property of Disney.

Item	S/1999
Wild Wing	$16.00
Wild Wing Christmas, LE 1998	$18.00
Wild Wing Talking	$15.00

Wild Wing Christmas

NASCAR® Beanie Racers

Front: Hamilton, Martin, Stricklin; Back: Rudd, Elliot, Green

This NASCAR bean bag car set is made by The Jones Group and PJ Toys. Collectors can find these bean bags at sports stores and gift shops like Hallmark. The Derrick Cope bean bag is the toughest to locate.

Item	W/1998	S/1999
Johnny Benson, #26 Cheerios	n/a	$8.00
Jeff Burton, #99 Exide Batteries	n/a	$8.00
Ward Burton, #22 MBNA	n/a	$8.00
Derrick Cope, #30 Gumout	n/a	$28.00
Dale Earnhardt, #3 GM Goodwrench	n/a	$9.00
Dale Earnhardt Jr., #3 AC Delco	n/a	$15.00
Bill Elliott, #94 McDonald's	$10.00	$8.00
Bill Elliott, #94 McDonald's gold	n/a	$12.00
Bill Elliott, #94 McDonald's, Mac Tonight	n/a	$12.00
David Green, #96 Caterpillar	$12.00	$8.00
Jeff Green, #46 First Union	n/a	$8.00
Bobby Hamilton, #4 Kodak	$10.00	$8.00
Bobby Labonte, #18 Interstate Batteries	n/a	$8.00
Chad Little, #97 John Deere	n/a	$8.00
Mark Martin, #6 Eagle One	n/a	$12.00
Mark Martin, #6 Valvoline	$15.00	$8.00
Ted Musgrave, #16 Primestar	n/a	$8.00
Jerry Nadeau, #13 First Plus	n/a	$8.00
Joe Nemechek, #42 Bell South	n/a	$8.00
Steve Park, #1 Pennzoil	n/a	$8.00
Ricky Rudd, #10 Tide	$10.00	$8.00
Hut Stricklin, #8 Circuit City	$10.00	$8.00
Rusty Wallace, #2	n/a	$11.00

NFL Coolbeans®

Front: Touchdown, Rah Rah; Back: Cleats, Tackle, Cheers, Pigskin

NFL Coolbeans have been made for every NFL team. They can be found in sports and other retail stores. TD the Dolphin was available only at the NFL Experience at the 1999 Super Bowl in Miami, and was limited to 7,500.

Item	W/1998	S/1999
Bucky the beaver	$8.00	$7.00
Cheers the frog	$8.00	$7.00
Chomps the Bulldog, TV Guide	$15.00	$15.00
Cleats the cow	$8.00	$7.00
Clyde the cow	$8.00	$7.00
Morris the moose	$8.00	$7.00
Pigskin the pig	$8.00	$7.00
Rah Rah the rhino	$8.00	$7.00
Rocket the rabbit	$8.00	$7.00
TD the Dolphin (LE)	n/a	$15.00
Tackle the elephant	$8.00	$7.00
Touchdown the lion	$8.00	$7.00
Tycoon the raccoon	$8.00	$7.00
Wizard the cat	$8.00	$7.00

Racing Horses® Beanys

Several special racing horse bean bags are available. Some of these were bought at http://www.churchill-down.com and others through the "Impressions of Saratoga" catalog.

Top: "Julie," "Black Eyed" Susan, 1998 Breeder's Cup; Bottom: Dashing Derby, Racing Rosey, Pegasus Pride

Item	W/1998	S/1999
Belmont		
1998 "Julie" Beanie Pony (R)	$22.00	$15.00
Breeders' Cup		
1998 Breeders' Cup	n/a	$15.00
Kentucky Derby		
1998 Dashing Derby (R)	$13.00	$16.00
1998 Racing Rosey (R)	$13.00	$16.00
1999 Backside Bob	n/a	$15.00
1999 Turfclub Tom	n/a	$15.00
1998 Pegasus Pride (KD Festival) (R)	$18.00	$15.00
1999 Penny the Pegasus (KD Festival)	n/a	$15.00
Preakness		
1998 "Black Eyed" Susan	$29.00	$45.00

Red Liners Bean Bag Race Cars

Mary Meyer-produced set of NASCAR bean bags.

Left: Jarrett, Earnhardt, Gordon

Item	W/1998	S/1999
Jeff Burton, #99	$18.00	$20.00
Dale Earnhardt, #3, black	$22.00	$20.00
Dale Earnhardt, #3, gold	n/a	$25.00
Dale Earnhardt, #3, red, Japan	n/a	$25.00
Dale Earnhardt Jr., #1, Japan	n/a	$25.00
Jeff Gordon, #24	$24.00	$20.00
Kenny Irwin, #28	$18.00	$20.00
Dale Jarrett, #88	$21.00	$20.00
Mark Martin, #6	$22.00	$20.00
Rusty Wallace, #2	$18.00	$20.00

Speedie Beanies

This cute set of 5-inch long, officially licensed NASCAR car bean bags is a real keeper. Produced by Team Up International and first available in 1999.

Item	S/1999
Dale Earnhardt, #3	$5.00
Jeff Gordon, #24	$5.00
Dale Jarrett, #88	$5.00
Terry Labonte, #5	$5.00
Mark Martin, #6	$5.00

Labonte, Jarrett, Earnhardt

Sydney 2000 (Olympics)

Three different mascot bean bags were created for the Sydney 2000 Summer Olympics. They are sold in Australia only, so you'll either need to have an overseas friend get them for you, or buy them on the secondary market.

Item	S/1999
Millie the Echidna	$10.00
Ollie the Kookaburra	$10.00
Syd the Platypus	$10.00

Millie, Ollie, Syd

World Cup® "Oranje" Lion Bean Bag

Mascot bean bag for the 1998 World Cup for the Holland team.

Item	W/1998	S/1999
Oranje	$10.00	$10.00

Ty®
Beanie Babies®

Regular,
Special Edition,
& Teenie
Beanie Babies®

Ty® Beanie Babies®
Regular, Special Edition, & Teenie Beanie Babies®

The Ty Inc. plush products depicted in this publication are the copyrighted property of Ty Inc., and all photographs of Ty's plush products in this publication are used by permission of Ty Inc. ©1999, Ty Inc.

The Beanie Baby section is broken into three categories: regular line Beanie Babies (those that are available through normal retail outlets), special edition Beanie Babies (those that are made for special events such as Broadway shows, the Beanie Babies Official Club, and sporting events), and Teenie Beanie Babies (McDonald's promotion).

Tag Identification

Some people are recognizing a 6th generation hang-tag. The mere difference between the 5th and "6th" style tag is that a narrower typestyle is used, and there are some slight spacing variations. In my opinion, these changes are not enough to warrant recognition of a new version hang-tag, and collectors seem to agree (albeit, most bean bag publications are recognizing the "6th generation" hang-tag).

Style 1 hang-tag (1994) The first Beanie Babies had a single-sided hang-tag. The front of the heart-shaped hang-tag has the letters "ty" in lower case in thin letters.

Style 2 hang-tag (1994-1995) The second hang-tag opened up like a book. The front was the same as Style 1.

Style 3 hang-tag (1995-1996) The third hang-tag has a re-designed heart shape and much larger and fatter "ty" letters on the front. The inside remained the same.

Style 4 hang-tag (1996-1997) A star with the words "Beanie Original Baby" was added to the front of the fourth hang-tag. Birthdates and poems were added on the inside of the tags.

Style 5 hang-tag (1997-present) The font (type style) was changed to a comic style.

Beanie Babies: Regular Line Beanie Babies

1997 Teddy™ the bear (R)
Style #4200
Released: 9-30-97

Born: 12-25-96
Retired: 12-31-97

Tag	S/1998	W/1998	S/1999
4th	$35.00	$45.00	$40.00
5th	$35.00	$40.00	$45.00

1998 Holiday Teddy™ (R)
Style #4204
Released: 9-30-98

Born: 12-25-98
Retired: 12-31-98

Tag	S/1999
5th	$42.00

1999 Signature Bear™
Style #4228
Released: 12-31-98

Born: n/a
Current

Tag	S/1999
5th	$10.00

Ally™ the alligator (R)
Style #4032
Released: 1994

Born: 3-14-94
Retired: 9-30-97

Tag	S/1998	W/1998	S/1999
1st	$350.00	$450.00	$425.00
2nd	$275.00	$230.00	$240.00
3rd	$175.00	$100.00	$165.00
4th	$45.00	$48.00	$48.00

Almond™ the beige bear
Style #4246
Released: 4-19-99

Born: 9-14-99
Current

Tag	S/1999
5th	$9.00

Amber™ the tabby cat
Style #4243
Released: 4-20-99

Born: 2-21-99
Current

Tag	S/1999
5th	$8.00

Ants™ the aardvark (R)
Style #4195
Released: 5-31-98

Born: 11-7-97
Retired: 12-31-98

Tag	W/1998	S/1999
5th	$8.00	$6.00

Baldy™ the bald eagle (R)
Style #4074
Released: 5-11-97

Born: 2-17-96
Retired: 5-1-98

Tag	S/1998	W/1998	S/1999
4th	$14.00	$15.00	$15.00
5th	$11.00	$15.00	$15.00

Batty™ the bat (R)
Style #4035
Released: 9-30-97
1st version: brown
2nd version: tie-dye

Born: 10-29-96
Retired: 3-31-99

Ver.-Tag	S/1998	W/1998	S/1999
1st-4th	$12.00	$9.00	$8.00
1st-5th	$8.00	$7.00	$8.00
2nd-5th	n/a	n/a	$9.00

Beak™ the kiwi bird
Style #4211
Released: 9-30-98

Born: 2-3-98
Current

Tag	S/1999
5th	$7.00

Bernie™ the St. Bernard (R)
Style #4109
Released: 1-1-97

Born: 10-3-96
Retired: 9-22-98

Tag	S/1998	W/1998	S/1999
4th	$8.00	$10.00	$8.00
5th	$7.00	$9.00	$7.00

Bessie™ the cow (R)
Style #4009
Released: 1995

Born: 6-27-95
Retired: 9-30-97

Tag	S/1998	W/1998	S/1999
3rd	$250.00	$115.00	$100.00
4th	$50.00	$60.00	$50.00

Blackie™ the bear (R)
Style #4011
Released: 1995

Born: 7-15-94
Retired: 9-15-98

Tag	S/1998	W/1998	S/1999
1st	$300.00	$375.00	$310.00
2nd	$235.00	$300.00	$175.00
3rd	$125.00	$100.00	$90.00
4th	$12.00	$18.00	$12.00
5th	$10.00	$18.00	$11.00

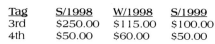

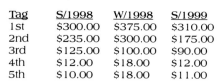

Blizzard™ the white tiger (R)
Style #4163
Released: 5-11-97

Born: 12-12-96
Retired: 5-1-98

Tag	S/1998	W/1998	S/1999
4th	$14.00	$14.00	$10.00
5th	$12.00	$12.00	$10.00

Bones™ the dog (R)
Style #4001
Released: 1994

Born: 1-18-94
Retired: 5-1-98

Tag	S/1998	W/1998	S/1999
1st	$325.00	$210.00	$240.00
2nd	$275.00	$140.00	$160.00
3rd	$150.00	$110.00	$60.00
4th	$11.00	$9.00	$12.00
5th	$9.00	$8.00	$10.00

Bongo™ the monkey (R)
Style #4067
Released: 1995

Born: 8-17-95
Retired: 12-31-98

1st version: "Nana" tags
2nd version: "Bongo" tags, tan tail
3rd version: "Bongo" tags, brown tail

Ver.-Tag	S/1998	W/1998	S/1999
1st-3rd	$3,600.00	$3,500.00	$3,300.00
2nd-3rd	$190.00	$150.00	$150.00
2nd-4th	$9.00	$8.00	$8.00
2nd-5th	$8.00	$7.00	$8.00
3rd-3rd	$150.00	$145.00	$110.00
3rd-4th	$75.00	$65.00	$45.00

Britannia™ the bear
UK exclusive
Style #4601
Released: 12-31-97

Born: 8-15-97
Retired: 7-26-99

Tag	S/1998	W/1998	S/1999
5th	$525.00	$300.00	$85.00

Bronty™ the brontosaurus (R)
Style #4085
Released: 1995

Born: n/a
Retired: 1996

Tag	S/1998	W/1998	S/1999
3rd	$1,400.00	$900.00	$600.00

Bruno™ the terrier (R)
Style #4183
Released: 12-31-97

Born: 9-9-97
Retired: 9-18-98

Tag	S/1998	W/1998	S/1999
5th	$8.00	$9.00	$8.00

Bubbles™ the fish (R)
Style #4078
Released: 1995

Born: 7-2-95
Retired: 5-11-97

Tag	S/1998	W/1998	S/1999
3rd	$270.00	$210.00	$225.00
4th	$200.00	$150.00	$150.00

Bucky™ the beaver (R)
Style #4016
Released: 1996

Born: 6-8-95
Retired: 12-31-97

Tag	S/1998	W/1998	S/1999
3rd	$110.00	$90.00	$100.00
4th	$27.00	$30.00	$32.00

Bumble™ the bee (R)
Style #4045
Released: 1995

Born: 10-16-95
Retired: 1996

Tag	S/1998	W/1998	S/1999
3rd	$660.00	$630.00	$350.00
4th	$670.00	$610.00	$325.00

Butch™ the bull terrier
Style #4227
Released: 12-31-98

Born: 10-2-98
Current

Tag	S/1999
5th	$8.00

Canyon™ the cougar
Style #4212
Released: 9-30-98

Born: 5-29-98
Current

Tag	S/1999
5th	$8.00

Caw™ the crow (R)
Style #4071
Released: 1995

Born: n/a
Retired: 1996

Tag	S/1998	W/1998	S/1999
3rd	$800.00	$660.00	$400.00

Cheeks™ the baboon
Style #4250
Released: 4-17-99

Born: 5-10-99
Current

Tag	S/1999
5th	$8.00

Chilly™ the polar bear (R)
Style #4012 Born: n/a
Released: 1994 Retired: 1995

Tag	S/1998	W/1998	S/1999
1st	$2,600.00	$2,200.00	$1,650.00
2nd	$2,500.00	$2,000.00	$1,500.00
3rd	$2,100.00	$1,800.00	$1,400.00

Chip™ the cat (R)
Style #4121 Born: 1-26-97
Released: 5-11-97 Retired: 3-31-99

Tag	S/1998	W/1998	S/1999
3rd	$10.00	$8.00	$9.00
4th	$8.00	$7.00	$8.00

Chocolate® the moose (R)
Style #4015 Born: 4-27-93
Released: 1994 Retired: 12-31-98

Tag	S/1998	W/1998	S/1999
1st	$1,200.00	$950.00	$625.00
2nd	$600.00	$400.00	$290.00
3rd	$175.00	$140.00	$100.00
4th	$12.00	$9.00	$9.00
5th	$9.00	$7.00	$8.00

Chops® the lamb (R)
Style #4019 Born: 5-3-96
Released: 1996 Retired: 1-1-97

Tag	S/1998	W/1998	S/1999
3rd	$280.00	$225.00	$255.00
4th	$210.00	$180.00	$125.00

Claude™ the crab (R)
Style #4083 Born: 9-3-96
Released: 5-11-97 Retired: 12-31-98

Tag	S/1998	W/1998	S/1999
4th	$17.00	$16.00	$12.00
5th	$8.00	$9.00	$10.00

Congo™ the gorilla (R)
Style #4160 Born: 11-9-96
Released: 1996 Retired: 12-31-98

Tag	S/1998	W/1998	S/1999
4th	$10.00	$9.00	$9.00
5th	$8.00	$8.00	$8.00

Coral™ the fish (R)
Style #4067
Released: 1995

Born: 3-2-95
Retired: 1-1-97

Tag	S/1998	W/1998	S/1999
3rd	$285.00	$240.00	$210.00
4th	$215.00	$215.00	$175.00

Crunch™ the shark (R)
Style #4130
Released: 1-1-97

Born: 1-13-96
Retired: 9-24-98

Tag	S/1998	W/1998	S/1999
4th	$8.00	$9.00	$8.00
5th	$6.00	$8.00	$6.00

Cubbie™ the bear (R)
Style #4010
Released: 1994
1st version: "Brownie" tags
2nd version: "Cubby" tags

Born: 11-14-96
Retired: 12-31-97

Ver.-Tag	S/1998	W/1998	S/1999
1st-1st	$4,200.00	$3,400.00	$2,100.00
2nd-1st	$1,100.00	$675.00	$650.00
2nd-2nd	$525.00	$410.00	$550.00
2nd-3rd	$225.00	$300.00	$215.00
2nd-4th	$16.00	$22.00	$20.00
2nd-5th	$16.00	$20.00	$20.00

Curly™ the bear (R)
Style #4052
Released: 1996

Born: 4-12-96
Retired: 12-31-98

Tag	S/1998	W/1998	S/1999
4th	$25.00	$18.00	$18.00
5th	$20.00	$12.00	$16.00

Daisy™ the cow (R)
Style #4067
Released: 1994

Born: 5-10-94
Retired: 9-15-98

Tag	S/1998	W/1998	S/1999
1st	$300.00	$300.00	$300.00
2nd	$285.00	$200.00	$275.00
3rd	$120.00	$90.00	$125.00
4th	$10.00	$10.00	$10.00
5th	$8.00	$8.00	$10.00

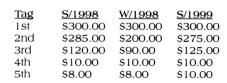

Derby™ the horse (R)
Style #4008
Released: 1995
1st version: fine mane
2nd version: coarse mane, no star
3rd version: coarse mane, star
4th version: fuzzy mane, star (current)

Born: 9-16-95
Retired: 5-26-99

Ver.-Tag	S/1998	W/1998	S/1999
1st-3rd	$4,000.00	$3,200.00	$2,500.00
2nd-3rd	$400.00	$200.00	$140.00
2nd-4th	$20.00	$20.00	$16.00
3rd-5th	$10.00	$8.00	$8.00
4th-5th	n/a	n/a	$8.00

Digger™ the crab (R)
Style #4027
Released: 1995
1st version: orange
2nd version: red

Born: 8-23-95
Retired: 5-11-97

Ver.-Tag	S/1998	W/1998	S/1999
1st-1st	$800.00	$950.00	$950.00
1st-2nd	$800.00	$800.00	$600.00
1st-3rd	$750.00	$800.00	$600.00
2nd-3rd	$200.00	$225.00	$225.00
2nd-4th	$125.00	$125.00	$100.00

Doby™ the doberman (R)
Style #4110
Released: 1-1-97

Born: 10-9-96
Retired: 12-31-98

Tag	S/1998	W/1998	S/1999
4th	$13.00	$8.00	$8.00
5th	$8.00	$7.00	$8.00

Doodle the rooster (R)
Style #4171
Released: 5-11-97

Born: 3-8-96
Retired: July 1997

Tag	S/1998	W/1998	S/1999
4th	$40.00	$45.00	$42.00

Dotty™ the dalmatian (R)
Style #4100
Released: 5-11-97

Born: 10-17-96
Retired: 12-31-98

Tag	S/1998	W/1998	S/1999
4th	$15.00	$10.00	$9.00
5th	$8.00	$9.00	$9.00

Early™ the robin
Style #4190
Released: 5-31-98

Born: 3-20-97
Current

Tag	W/1998	S/1999
5th	$8.00	$7.00

Ears™ the bunny (R)
Style #4018
Released: 1996

Born: 4-18-95
Retired: 5-1-98

Tag	S/1998	W/1998	S/1999
3rd	$115.00	$115.00	$100.00
4th	$12.00	$15.00	$15.00
5th	$8.00	$15.00	$15.00

Echo™ the dolphin (R)
Style #4180
Released: 5-11-97
1st version: "Waves" tags
2nd version: "Echo" tags

Born: 12-21-96
Retired: 5-1-98

Ver.-Tag	S/1998	W/1998	S/1999
1-4th	$15.00	$12.00	$14.00
2-4th	$10.00	$11.00	$12.00
2-5th	$8.00	$10.00	$12.00

Eggbert™ the baby chick
Style #4232
Released: 12-31-98

Born: 4-10-98
Retired: 7-28-99

Tag	S/1999
5th	$10.00

Erin™ the bear (R)
Style #4186
Released: 1-31-98

Born: 3-17-97
Retired: 5-21-99

Tag	S/1998	W/1998	S/1999
5th	$75.00	$30.00	$12.00

Eucalyptus™ the koala
Style #4240
Released: 4-8-99

Born: 4-28-99
Current

Tag	S/1999
5th	n/a

Ewey™ the lamb (R)
Style #4219
Released: 12-31-98

Born: 3-1-98
Retired: 7-19-99

Tag	S/1999
5th	$7.00

Fetch™ the golden retriever (R)
Style #4189
Released: 5-31-98

Born: 2-4-97
Retired: 12-31-98

Tag	W/1998	S/1999
5th	$8.00	$10.00

Flash™ the dolphin (R)
Style #4021   Born: 5-13-93
Released: 1994   Retired: 5-11-97

Tag	S/1998	W/1998	S/1999
1st	$500.00	$425.00	$425.00
2nd	$425.00	$300.00	$300.00
3rd	$200.00	$180.00	$200.00
4th	$100.00	$100.00	$110.00

Fleece™ the lamb (R)
Style #4125   Born: 3-21-96
Released: 1-1-97   Retired: 12-31-98

Tag	S/1998	W/1998	S/1999
4th	$10.00	$10.00	$9.00
5th	$8.00	$8.00	$9.00

Flip™ the cat (R)
Style #4012   Born: 2-28-95
Released: 1996   Retired: 9-30-97

Tag	S/1998	W/1998	S/1999
3rd	$150.00	$110.00	$125.00
4th	$26.00	$32.00	$30.00

Floppity™ the bunny (R)
Style #4118   Born: 5-28-96
Released: 1-1-97   Retired: 5-1-98

Tag	S/1998	W/1998	S/1999
4th	$12.00	$16.00	$14.00
5th	$8.00	$14.00	$14.00

Flutter™ the butterfly (R)
Style #4043   Born: n/a
Released: 1995   Retired: 1996

Tag	S/1998	W/1998	S/1999
3rd	$1,200.00	$925.00	$650.00

Fortune™ the panda bear
Style #4196   Born: 12-6-97
Released: 5-31-98   Current

Tag	W/1998	S/1999
5th	$22.00	$9.00

Freckles™ the leopard (R)
Style #4066   Born: 6-3-96
Released: 1996   Retired: 12-31-98

Tag	S/1998	W/1998	S/1999
4th	$10.00	$12.00	$9.00
5th	$8.00	$8.00	$9.00

Fuzz™ the bear
Style #4237
Released: 12-31-98

Born: 7-23-98
Current

Tag	S/1999
5th	$22.00

Garcia the bear (R)
Style #4051
Released: 1996

Born: 8-1-95
Retired: 5-11-97

Tag	S/1998	W/1998	S/1999
3rd	$270.00	$225.00	$250.00
4th	$180.00	$170.00	$150.00

Germania™ the bear
Germany exclusive
Style #4236
Released: 12-31-98

Born: 10-3-98
Current

Tag	S/1999
5th	$250.00

Gigi™ the poodle
Style #4191
Released: 5-31-98

Born: 4-7-97
Current

Tag	W/1998	S/1999
5th	$10.00	$8.00

Glory™ the bear (R)
Style #4188
Released: 5-31-98

Born: 7-4-97
Retired: 12-31-98

Tag	W/1998	S/1999
5th	$40.00	$25.00

Goatee™ the goat
Style #4235
Released: 12-31-98

Born: 11-4-98
Current

Tag	S/1999
5th	$9.00

Gobbles™ the turkey (R)
Style #4034
Released: 9-30-97

Born: 11-27-96
Retired: 3-31-99

Tag	S/1998	W/1998	S/1999
4th	$15.00	$15.00	$12.00
5th	$8.00	$8.00	$10.00

Goldie™ the fish (R)
Style #4023
Released: 1995

Born: 11-14-94
Retired: 12-31-97

Tag	S/1998	W/1998	S/1999
1st	$175.00	$400.00	$400.00
2nd	$150.00	$250.00	$250.00
3rd	$130.00	$115.00	$125.00
4th	$35.00	$35.00	$38.00
5th	$35.00	$40.00	$38.00

Goochy™ the jellyfish
Style #4230
Released: 12-31-98
1st version: greenish
2nd version: tie-dye

Born: 11-18-98
Current

Ver.-Tag	S/1999
1st-5th	$9.00
2nd-5th	$10.00

Gracie™ the swan (R)
Style #4126
Released: 1-1-97

Born: 6-17-96
Retired: 5-1-98

Tag	S/1998	W/1998	S/1999
4th	$9.00	$12.00	$13.00
5th	$8.00	$12.00	$12.00

Grunt™ the razorback (R)
Style #4092
Released: 1996

Born: 7-19-95
Retired: 5-11-97

Tag	S/1998	W/1998	S/1999
3rd	$300.00	$240.00	$240.00
4th	$150.00	$175.00	$150.00

Halo™ the angel bear
Style #4208
Released: 9-30-98

Born: 8-31-98
Current

Tag	S/1999
5th	$10.00

Happy™ the hippo (R)
Style #4061
Released: 1995
1st version: gray
2nd version: lavender

Born: 2-25-94
Retired: 5-1-98

Ver.-Tag	S/1998	W/1998	S/1999
1st-1st	$1,200.00	$950.00	$700.00
1st-2nd	$850.00	$850.00	$500.00
1st-3rd	$850.00	$800.00	$425.00
2nd-3rd	$150.00	$175.00	$175.00
2nd-4th	$10.00	$20.00	$22.00
2nd-5th	$8.00	$18.00	$20.00

Hippie™ the bunny (R)
Style #4218
Released: 12-31-98

Born: 5-4-98
Retired: 7-12-99

Tag	S/1999
5th	$8.00

Hippity™ the bunny (R)
Style #4119
Released: 1-1-97

Born: 6-1-96
Retired: 5-1-98

Tag	S/1998	W/1998	S/1999
4th	$12.00	$16.00	$16.00
5th	$8.00	$14.00	$14.00

Hissy™ the snake (R)
Style #4185
Released: 12-31-97

Born: 4-4-97
Retired: 3-31-99

Tag	S/1998	W/1998	S/1999
5th	$12.00	$7.00	$8.00

Hoot™ the owl (R)
Style #4073
Released: 1996

Born: 8-9-95
Retired: 9-30-97

Tag	S/1998	W/1998	S/1999
3rd	$110.00	$95.00	$90.00
4th	$35.00	$38.00	$40.00

Hope™ the praying bear
Style #4223
Released: 12-31-98

Born: 3-23-98
Current

Tag	S/1999
5th	$8.00

Hoppity™ the bunny (R)
Style #4117
Released: 1-1-97

Born: 4-3-96
Retired: 5-1-98

Tag	S/1998	W/1998	S/1999
4th	$12.00	$14.00	$14.00
5th	$8.00	$14.00	$14.00

Humphrey™ the camel (R)
Style #4060
Released: 1994

Born: n/a
Retired: 1995

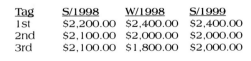

Tag	S/1998	W/1998	S/1999
1st	$2,200.00	$2,400.00	$2,400.00
2nd	$2,100.00	$2,000.00	$2,000.00
3rd	$2,100.00	$1,800.00	$2,000.00

Iggy™ the iguana (R)
Style #4038
Released: 12-31-97
1st version: tie-dye, no tongue
2nd version: tie-dye, with tongue
3rd version: blue

Born: 8-12-97
Retired: 3-31-99

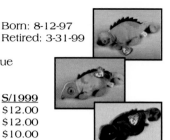

Ver.-Tag	S/1998	W/1998	S/1999
1st-5th	$9.00	$8.00	$12.00
2nd-5th	n/a	$8.00	$12.00
3rd-5th	n/a	$10.00	$10.00

Inch™ the worm (R)
Style #4044
Released: 1995
1st version: felt antennas
2nd version: yarn antennas

Born: 9-3-95
Retired: 5-1-98

Ver.-Tag	S/1998	W/1998	S/1999
1st-3rd	$200.00	$200.00	$200.00
1st-4th	$200.00	$180.00	$110.00
2nd-4th	$12.00	$20.00	$21.00
2nd-5th	$10.00	$15.00	$18.00

Inky™ the octopus (R)
Style #4028
Released: 1994
1st version: tan, no mouth
2nd version: tan, with mouth
3rd version: pink

Born: 11-29-94
Retired: 5-1-98

Ver.-Tag	S/1998	W/1998	S/1999
1st-1st	$900.00	$900.00	$900.00
1st-2nd	$880.00	$875.00	$875.00
2nd-2nd	$800.00	$800.00	$800.00
2nd-3rd	$700.00	$600.00	$600.00
3rd-3rd	$200.00	$225.00	$200.00
3rd-4th	$10.00	$26.00	$26.00
3rd-5th	$8.00	$25.00	$22.00

Jabber™ the parrot
Style #4197
Released: 5-31-98

Born: 10-10-97
Current

Tag	W/1998	S/1999
5th	$9.00	$7.00

Jake™ the mallard duck
Style #4199
Released: 5-31-98

Born: 4-16-97
Current

Tag	W/1998	S/1999
5th	$9.00	$8.00

Jolly™ the walrus (R)
Style #4082
Released: 5-11-97

Born: 12-2-96
Retired: 5-1-98

Tag	S/1998	W/1998	S/1999
4th	$11.00	$17.00	$16.00
5th	$10.00	$14.00	$15.00

Kicks™ the soccer bear
Style #4229
Released: 12-31-98

Born: 8-16-98
Current

Tag	S/1999
5th	$10.00

Kiwi™ the toucan (R)
Style #4070
Released: 1995

Born: 9-16-95
Retired: 1-1-97

Tag	S/1998	W/1998	S/1999
3rd	$300.00	$275.00	$275.00
4th	$255.00	$180.00	$150.00

Knuckles™ the pig
Style #4247
Released: 4-14-99

Born: 3-25-99
Current

Tag	S/1999
5th	$16.00

Kuku™ the cockatoo
Style #4192
Released: 5-31-98

Born: 1-5-97
Current

Tag	W/1998	S/1999
5th	$11.00	$7.00

Lefty™ the donkey (R)
Style #4057
Released: 1996

Born: 7-4-96
Retired: 1-1-97

Tag	S/1998	W/1998	S/1999
4th	$300.00	$300.00	$190.00

Legs™ the frog (R)
Style #4020
Released: 1994

Born: 4-25-93
Retired: 9-30-97

Tag	S/1998	W/1998	S/1999
1st	$400.00	$450.00	$450.00
2nd	$325.00	$375.00	$350.00
3rd	$100.00	$110.00	$110.00
4th	$18.00	$18.00	$18.00

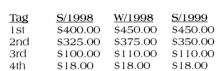

Libearty™ the bear (R)
Style #4057
Released: 1996

Born: Summer '96
Retired: 1-1-97

Tag	S/1998	W/1998	S/1999
4th	$400.00	$375.00	$300.00

Lizzy® the lizard (R)
Style #4033
Released: 1995
1st version: tie-dye
2nd version: blue

Born: 5-11-95
Retired: 12-31-97

Ver.-Tag	S/1998	W/1998	S/1999
1st-3rd	$1,300.00	$1,300.00	$750.00
2nd-3rd	$275.00	$180.00	$200.00
2nd-4th	$15.00	$18.00	$24.00
2nd-5th	$18.00	$15.00	$20.00

Loosy™ the Canada goose
Style #4206
Released: 9-30-98

Born: 3-29-98
Current

Tag	S/1999
5th	$8.00

Lucky™ the ladybug (R)
Style #4040
Released: 1994
1st version: 7 felt spots
2nd version: 21 spots
3rd version: 11 spots

Born: 5-1-95
Retired: 5-1-98

Ver.-Tag	S/1998	W/1998	S/1999
1st-1st	$600.00	$475.00	$500.00
1-2nd	$500.00	$375.00	$400.00
1st-3rd	$300.00	$250.00	$200.00
2nd-4th	$600.00	$450.00	$400.00
3rd-4th	$14.00	$18.00	$15.00
3rd-5th	$10.00	$16.00	$15.00

Luke™ the Lab
Style #4214
Released: 12-31-98

Born: 6-15-98
Current

Tag	S/1999
5th	$10.00

Mac™ the cardinal
Style #4225
Released: 12-31-98

Born: 6-10-98
Current

Tag	S/1999
5th	$10.00

Magic™ the dragon (R)
Style #4088
Released: 1995
1st version: hot pink thread
2nd version: light pink thread

Born: 9-5-95
Retired: 12-31-97

Ver.-Tag	S/1998	W/1998	S/1999
1st-4th	$75.00	$85.00	$50.00
2nd-3rd	$150.00	$150.00	$175.00
2nd-4th	$40.00	$40.00	$40.00

Manny™ the manatee (R)
Style #4081
Released: 1996

Born: 6-8-95
Retired: 5-11-97

Tag	S/1998	W/1998	S/1999
3rd	$230.00	$210.00	$225.00
4th	$180.00	$150.00	$150.00

Maple™ the Canadian bear
Canada exclusive
Style #4600
Released: 1-1-97
1st version: "Pride" tags
2nd version: "Maple" tags

Born: 7-1-96
Current

Ver.-Tag	S/1998	W/1998	S/1999
1st-4th	$650.00	$575.00	$425.00
2nd-4th	$300.00	$245.00	$110.00
2nd-5th	$300.00	$225.00	$100.00

Mel™ the koala (R)
Style #4162
Released: 1-1-97

Born: 1-15-96
Retired: 3-31-99

Tag	S/1998	W/1998	S/1999
4th	$8.00	$9.00	$10.00
5th	$7.00	$7.00	$9.00

Millennium™ the bear
Style #4226
Released: 12-31-98

Born: 1-1-99
Current

Tag	S/1999
5th	$14.00

Mooch™ the spider monkey
Style #4224
Released: 12-31-98

Born: 8-1-98
Current

Tag	S/1999
5th	$8.00

Mystic™ the unicorn (R)
Style #4007

Born: 5-21-94

Released: 1994

Retired: 5-18-99

1st version: fine mane
2nd version: coarse mane, gold horn
3rd version: coarse mane, iridescent horn
4th version: fuzzy rainbow mane, iridescent horn (current)

Ver.-Tag	S/1998	W/1998	S/1999
1st-1st	$700.00	$500.00	$500.00
1st-2nd	$625.00	$440.00	$425.00
1st-3rd	$500.00	$375.00	$300.00
2nd-3rd	$125.00	$115.00	$75.00
2nd-4th	$30.00	$34.00	$25.00
2nd-5th	$20.00	$30.00	$25.00
3rd-4th	$17.00	$12.00	$10.00
3rd-5th	$8.00	$8.00	$8.00
4th-5th	n/a	n/a	$10.00

Nanook™ the husky (R)
Style #4104

Born: 11-21-96

Released: 5-11-97

Retired: 3-31-99

Tag	S/1998	W/1998	S/1999
4th	$15.00	$12.00	$10.00
5th	$9.00	$8.00	$8.00

Neon™ the seahorse
Style #4239

Born: 4-1-99

Released: 4-8-99

Current

Tag	S/1999
5th	$8.00

Nibbler™ the rabbit (R)
Style #4216

Born: 4-6-98

Released: 12-31-98

Retired: 7-9-99

Tag	S/1999
5th	$7.00

Nibbly™ the Rabbit (R)
Style #4217

Born: 5-7-98

Released: 12-31-98

Retired: 7-20-99

Tag	S/1999
5th	$7.00

Nip™ the cat (R)
Style #4003

Born: 3-6-94

Released: 1995

Retired: 12-31-97

1st version: white face, belly
2nd version: all gold
3rd version: gold face, white paws

Ver.-Tag	S/1998	W/1998	S/1999
1st-2nd	$500.00	$550.00	$700.00
1st-3rd	$450.00	$500.00	$600.00
2nd-3rd	$900.00	$800.00	$800.00
3rd-3rd	$300.00	$225.00	$260.00
3rd-4th	$20.00	$20.00	$18.00
3rd-5th	$20.00	$20.00	$18.00

Nuts™ the squirrel (R)
Style #4114
Released: 1-1-97

Born: 1-21-96
Retired: 12-31-98

Tag	S/1998	W/1998	S/1999
4th	$9.00	$8.00	$10.00
5th	$7.00	$7.00	$10.00

Osito™ the Mexican bear
Style #4244
Released: 4-17-99

Born: 2-5-99
Current

Tag	S/1999
5th	$24.00

Patti® the platypus (R)
Style #4025
Released: 1994
1st version: deep magenta
2nd version: magenta

Born: 1-6-93
Retired: 5-1-98

Ver.-Tag	S/1998	W/1998	S/1999
1st-1st	$1,500.00	$1,000.00	$1,000.00
1st-2nd	$1,000.00	$800.00	$875.00
1st-3rd	$700.00	$650.00	$475.00
2nd-3rd	$300.00	$375.00	$175.00
2nd-4th	$18.00	$18.00	$25.00
2nd-5th	$20.00	$18.00	$22.00

Paul™ the walrus
Style #4248
Released: 4-9-99

Born: 2-23-99
Current

Tag	S/1999
5th	$9.00

Peace™ the tie-dye bear (R)
Style #4053
Released: 5-11-97

Born: 2-1-96
Retired: 7-14-99

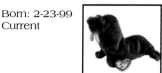

Tag	S/1998	W/1998	S/1999
4th	$50.00	$32.00	$30.00
5th	$50.00	$26.00	$12.00

Pecan™ the gold bear
Style #4251
Released: 4-8-99

Born: 4-15-99
Current

Tag	S/1999
5th	$10.00

Peanut™ the elephant (R)
Style #4062
Released: 1995
1st version: dark blue
2nd version: light blue

Born: 1-25-95
Retired: 5-1-98

Ver.-Tag	S/1998	W/1998	S/1999
1st-3rd	$4,800.00	$3,600.00	$3,650.00
2nd-3rd	$750.00	$800.00	$625.00
2nd-4th	$10.00	$16.00	$18.00
2nd-5th	$8.00	$18.00	$18.00

Peking™ the panda (R)
Style #4013
Released: 1994

Born: n/a
Retired: 1995

Tag	S/1998	W/1998	S/1999
1st	$2,400.00	$2,200.00	$1,700.00
2nd	$2,100.00	$2,100.00	$1,500.00
3rd	$2,000.00	$2,200.00	$1,400.00

Pinchers™ the lobster (R)
Style #4026
Released: 1994
1st version: "Punchers" tag
2nd version: "Pinchers" tag

Born: 6-19-93
Retired: 5-1-98

Ver.-Tag	S/1998	W/1998	S/1999
1st-1st	$3,400.00	$3,700.00	$3,500.00
2nd-1st	$1,000.00	$900.00	$750.00
2nd-2nd	$800.00	$700.00	$400.00
2nd-3rd	$175.00	$90.00	$90.00
2nd-4th	$10.00	$20.00	$15.00
2nd-5th	$8.00	$16.00	$14.00

Pinky™ the flamingo (R)
Style #4072
Released: 1995

Born: 2-13-95
Retired: 12-31-98

Tag	S/1998	W/1998	S/1999
3rd	$185.00	$200.00	$75.00
4th	$10.00	$11.00	$10.00
5th	$8.00	$7.00	$9.00

Pouch™ the kangaroo (R)
Style #4161
Released: 1-1-97

Born: 11-6-96
Retired: 3-31-99

Tag	S/1998	W/1998	S/1999
4th	$12.00	$11.00	$9.00
5th	$12.00	$7.00	$8.00

Pounce™ the cat (R)
Style #4122
Released: 12-31-97

Born: 8-28-97
Retired: 3-31-99

Tag	S/1998	W/1998	S/1999
5th	$8.00	$7.00	$8.00

Prance™ the cat (R)
Style #4123
Released: 12-31-97

Born: 11-20-97
Retired: 3-31-99

Tag	S/1998	W/1998	S/1999
5th	$10.00	$7.00	$8.00

Prickles™ the hedgehog
Style #4220
Released: 12-31-98

Born: 2-19-98
Current

Tag	S/1999
5th	$7.00

Princess™ (R)
Style #4300
Released: 10-29-97
1st version: P.V.C. pellets
2nd version: P.E. pellets

Born: n/a
Retired: 4-13-99

Ver.-Tag	S/1998	W/1998	S/1999
1st-5th	$125.00	$90.00	$68.00
2nd-5th	$75.00	$35.00	$12.00

Puffer™ the puffin
Style #4181
Released: 12-31-97

Born: 11-3-97
Current

Tag	S/1998	W/1998	S/1999
5th	$10.00	$12.00	$7.00

Pugsly™ the pug dog (R)
Style #4106
Released: 5-11-97

Born: 5-2-96
Retired: 3-31-99

Tag	S/1998	W/1998	S/1999
4th	$10.00	$8.00	$9.00
5th	$8.00	$8.00	$8.00

Pumkin™ the Pumpkin (R)
Style #4206
Released: 9-30-98

Born: 10-31-98
Retired: 12-31-98

Tag	S/1999
5th	$17.00

Quackers™ the duck (R)
Style #4024
Released: 1994
1st version: no wings (dis. 1995)
2nd version: wings

Born: 4-19-94
Retired: 5-1-98

Ver.-Tag	S/1998	W/1998	S/1999
1st-1st	$3,500.00	$2,100.00	$1,800.00
1st-2nd	$2,800.00	$1,800.00	$1,650.00
2nd-2nd	$600.00	$625.00	$500.00
2nd-3rd	$140.00	$85.00	$115.00
2nd-4th	$10.00	$12.00	$12.00
2nd-5th	$10.00	$12.00	$12.00

Radar™ the bat (R)
Style #4091   Born: 10-30-95
Released: 1995   Retired: 5-11-97

Tag	S/1998	W/1998	S/1999
3rd	$240.00	$185.00	$220.00
4th	$150.00	$160.00	$130.00

Rainbow™ the chameleon (R)
Style #4037   Born: 10-14-97
Released: 12-31-97   Retired: 3-31-99
1st version: blue, no tongue
2nd version: blue, tongue
3rd version: tie-dye

Ver.-Tag	S/1998	W/1998	S/1999
1st-5th	$9.00	$8.00	$10.00
2nd-5th	n/a	$8.00	$10.00
3rd-5th	n/a	$12.00	$9.00

Rex™ the tyrannosaurus (R)
Style #4086   Born: n/a
Released: 1995   Retired: 1996

Tag	S/1998	W/1998	S/1999
3rd	$900.00	$725.00	$625.00

Righty™ the elephant (R)
Style #4086   Born: 7-4-96
Released: 1996   Retired: 1-1-97

Tag	S/1998	W/1998	S/1999
4th	$300.00	$275.00	$200.00

Ringo™ the raccoon (R)
Style #4014   Born: 7-14-95
Released: 1996   Retired: 9-16-98

Tag	S/1998	W/1998	S/1999
3rd	$90.00	$75.00	$75.00
4th	$10.00	$12.00	$9.00
5th	$7.00	$9.00	$9.00

Roam™ the buffalo
Style #4209   Born: 9-27-98
Released: 9-30-98   Current

Tag	S/1999
5th	$11.00

Roary™ the lion (R)
Style #4069
Released: 5-11-97

Born: 2-20-96
Retired: 12-31-98

Tag	S/1998	W/1998	S/1999
4th	$9.00	$9.00	$8.00
5th	$7.00	$7.00	$8.00

Rocket™ the blue jay
Style #4202
Released: 5-31-98

Born: 3-12-97
Current

Tag	W/1998	S/1999
5th	$10.00	$10.00

Rover™ the dog (R)
Style #4101
Released: 1996

Born: 5-30-96
Retired: 5-1-98

Tag	S/1998	W/1998	S/1999
4th	$10.00	$20.00	$20.00
5th	$10.00	$18.00	$20.00

Sammy™ the bear
Style #4215
Released: 12-31-98

Born: 6-23-98
Current

Tag	S/1999
5th	$9.00

Santa™
Style #4203
Released: 9-30-98

Born: 12-6-98
Retired: 12-31-98

Tag	S/1999
5th	$18.00

Scat™ the cat
Style #4231
Released: 12-31-98

Born: 5-27-98
Current

Tag	S/1999
5th	$7.00

Schweetheart™ the orangutan
Style #4252
Released: 4-11-99

Born: 1-23-99
Current

Tag	S/1999
5th	$10.00

Scoop™ the pelican (R)
Style #4107
Released: 1996

Born: 7-1-96
12-31-98

Tag	S/1998	W/1998	S/1999
4th	$12.00	$8.00	$9.00
5th	$8.00	$7.00	$8.00

Scorch™ the Dragon
Style #4210
Released: 9-30-98

Born: 7-31-98
Current

Tag	S/1999
5th	$8.00

Scottie™ the Dog (R)
Style #4102
Released: 1996

Born: 6-15-96
Retired: 5-1-98

Tag	S/1998	W/1998	S/1999
4th	$14.00	$20.00	$21.00
5th	$12.00	$18.00	$20.00

Seamore™ the seal (R)
Style #4029
Released: 1994

Born: 12-14-96
Retired: 9-30-97

Tag	S/1998	W/1998	S/1999
1st	$500.00	$550.00	$500.00
2nd	$400.00	$425.00	$400.00
3rd	$225.00	$210.00	$125.00
4th	$175.00	$140.00	$70.00

Seaweed™ the otter (R)
Style #4080
Released: 1996

Born: 3-19-96
Retired: 9-18-98

Tag	S/1998	W/1998	S/1999
3rd	$110.00	$210.00	$75.00
4th	$10.00	$32.00	$15.00
5th	$8.00	$18.00	$12.00

Silver™ the gray tabby
Style #4242
Released: 4/21/99

Born: 2-11-99
Current

Tag	S/1999
5th	$10.00

Slippery™ the seal
Style #4222
Released: 12-31-98

Born: 1-17-98
Current

Tag	S/1999
5th	$8.00

Slither™ the snake (R)
Style #4031
Released: 1994

Born: n/a
Retired: 1995

Tag	S/1998	W/1998	S/1999
1st	$2,100.00	$2,400.00	$1,275.00
2nd	$2,100.00	$2,300.00	$1,200.00
3rd	$2,000.00	$2,350.00	$1,200.00

Sly™ the fox (R)
Style #4115
Released: 1996
1st version: brown belly
2nd version: white belly

Born: 9-12-96
Retired: 9-22-98

Ver.-Tag	S/1998	W/1998	S/1999
1st-4th	$200.00	$180.00	$125.00
2nd-4th	$10.00	$11.00	$10.00
2nd-5th	$8.00	$9.00	$10.00

Smoochy™ the frog (R)
Style #4039
Released: 12-31-97
1st version: string mouth
2nd version: felt mouth

Born: 10-1-97
Retired: 3-31-99

Ver.-Tag	S/1998	W/1998	S/1999
1st-5th	$7.00	$9.00	$9.00
2nd-5th	n/a	$7.00	$9.00

Snip™ the cat (R)
Style #4120
Released: 1-1-97

Born: 10-22-96
Retired: 12-31-98

Tag	S/1998	W/1998	S/1999
4th	$11.00	$10.00	$8.00
5th	$7.00	$7.00	$8.00

Snort® the bull (R)
Style #4002
Released: 1-1-97

Born: 5-15-95
Retired: 9-15-98

Tag	S/1998	W/1998	S/1999
4th	$10.00	$9.00	$10.00
5th	$8.00	$8.00	$9.00

Snowball™ the snowman (R)
Style #4201
Released: 9-30-97

Born: 12-22-96
Retired: 12-31-97

Tag	S/1998	W/1998	S/1999
4th	$30.00	$35.00	$24.00

Spangle™ the American bear
Style #4245
Released: 4-24-99

Born: 6-14-99
Current

Tag	S/1999
5th	$22.00

Sparky the dalmatian (R)
Style #4100
Released: 1996

Born: 2-27-96
Retired: 5-11-97

Tag	S/1998	W/1998	S/1999
4th	$170.00	$145.00	$95.00

Speedy® the turtle (R)
Style #4030
Released: 1994

Born: 8-14-94
Retired: 9-30-97

Tag	S/1998	W/1998	S/1999
1st	$700.00	$625.00	$400.00
2nd	$400.00	$225.00	$325.00
3rd	$105.00	$90.00	$72.00
4th	$24.00	$30.00	$24.00

Spike™ the rhino (R)
Style #4060
Released: 1996

Born: 8-13-96
Retired: 12-31-98

Tag	S/1998	W/1998	S/1999
4th	$11.00	$12.00	$10.00
5th	$8.00	$7.00	$9.00

Spinner™ the spider (R)
Style #4036
Released: 9-30-97

Born: 10-28-96
Retired: 9-18-98

Tag	S/1998	W/1998	S/1999
4th	$10.00	$11.00	$10.00
5th	$7.00	$10.00	$10.00

Splash™ the whale (R)
Style #4022
Released: 1994

Born: 7-8-93
Retired: 5-11-97

Tag	S/1998	W/1998	S/1999
1st	$860.00	$625.00	$475.00
2nd	$400.00	$350.00	$300.00
3rd	$200.00	$155.00	$145.00
4th	$100.00	$110.00	$80.00

Spooky™ the ghost (R)
Style #4090
Released: 1995
1st version: "Spook" tag
2nd version: "Spooky" tag

Born: 10-31-95
Retired: 12-31-97

Ver.-Tag	S/1998	W/1998	S/1999
1st-3rd	$425.00	$425.00	$450.00
2nd-3rd	$220.00	$135.00	$150.00
2nd-4th	$35.00	$35.00	$28.00

Spot™ the dog (R)
Style #4000
Released: 1994
1st version: no spot on back
2nd version: spot on back

Born: 1-3-93
Retired: 9-30-97

Ver.-Tag	S/1998	W/1998	S/1999
1st-1st	$2,400.00	$2,000.00	$1,850.00
1st-2nd	$2,200.00	$1,800.00	$1,700.00
2nd-2nd	$700.00	$380.00	$450.00
2nd-3rd	$125.00	$175.00	$170.00
2nd-4th	$50.00	$50.00	$45.00

Spunky™ the cocker spaniel (R)
Style #4184
Released: 12-31-97

Born: 1-14-97
Retired: 3-31-99

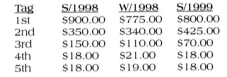

Tag	S/1998	W/1998	S/1999
5th	$9.00	$8.00	$9.00

Squealer™ the pig (R)
Style #4005
Released: 1994

Born: 4-23-93
Retired: 5-1-98

Tag	S/1998	W/1998	S/1999
1st	$900.00	$775.00	$800.00
2nd	$350.00	$340.00	$425.00
3rd	$150.00	$110.00	$70.00
4th	$18.00	$21.00	$18.00
5th	$18.00	$19.00	$18.00

Steg™ the stegosaurus (R)
Style #4087
Released: 1995

Born: n/a
Retired: 1996

Tag	S/1998	W/1998	S/1999
3rd	$1,200.00	$850.00	$745.00

Stilts™ the stork (R)
Style #4221
Released: 12-31-98

Born: 6-16-98
Retired: 5-31-99

Tag	S/1999
5th	$7.00

Sting™ the ray (R)
Style #4077
Released: 1995

Born: 8-27-95
Retired: 1-1-97

Tag	S/1998	W/1998	S/1999
3rd	$270.00	$275.00	$275.00
4th	$200.00	$200.00	$150.00

Stinger™ the scorpion (R)
Style #4193
Released: 5-31-98

Born: 9-29-97
Retired: 12-31-98

Tag	W/1998	S/1999
5th	$8.00	$7.00

Stinky™ the skunk (R)
Style #4017
Released: 1995

Born: 2-13-95
Retired: 9-28-98

Tag	S/1998	W/1998	S/1999
3rd	$90.00	$155.00	$75.00
4th	$10.00	$18.00	$12.00
5th	$8.00	$12.00	$12.00

Stretch™ the ostrich (R)
Style #4182
Released: 12-31-97

Born: 9-21-97
Retired: 3-31-99

Tag	S/1998	W/1998	S/1999
5th	$10.00	$8.00	$9.00

Stripes™ the tiger (R)
Style #4065
Released: 1995
1st version: orange, black stripes, fuzzy belly
2nd version: orange with black stripes
3rd version: tan with black stripes

Born: 6-11-95
Retired: 5-1-98

Ver.-Tag	S/1998	W/1998	S/1999
1st-3rd	$1,200.00	$1,150.00	$1,000.00
2nd-3rd	$400.00	$325.00	$400.00
3rd-4th	$11.00	$16.00	$15.00
3rd-5th	$10.00	$14.00	$12.00

Strut® the rooster (R)
Style #4171
Released: 7-12-97

Born: 3-8-96
Retired: 3-31-99

Tag	S/1998	W/1998	S/1999
4th	$13.00	$9.00	$9.00
5th	$11.00	$8.00	$9.00

Swirly™ the snail
Style #4249
Released: 4-14-99

Born: 3-10-99
Current

Tag	S/1999
5th	$8.00

Tabasco the bull (R)
Style #4002
Released: 1995

Born: 5-15-95
Retired: 1-1-97

Tag	S/1998	W/1998	S/1999
3rd	$275.00	$225.00	$190.00
4th	$200.00	$175.00	$140.00

Tank™ the armadillo (R)
Style #4031
Released: 1995
1st version: no shell, 7 lines
2nd version: no shell, 9 lines
3rd version: with shell

Born: 2-22-95
Retired: 9-30-97

Ver.-Tag	S/1998	W/1998	S/1999
1st-3rd	$200.00	$170.00	$200.00
1st-4th	$200.00	$170.00	$150.00
2nd-4th	$300.00	$260.00	$275.00
3rd-4th	$70.00	$85.00	$65.00

Teddy™ the bear (R)
Brown, new face
Style #4050
Released: 1995

Born: 11-28-95
Retired: 9-30-97

Tag	S/1998	W/1998	S/1999
2nd	$1,600.00	$1,000.00	$1,000.00
3rd	$400.00	$350.00	$500.00
4th	$85.00	$100.00	$85.00

Teddy™ the bear (R)
Brown, old face
Style #4050
Released: 1994

Born: n/a
Retired: 1995

Tag	S/1998	W/1998	S/1999
1st	$3,300.00	$2,400.00	$2,100.00
2nd	$3,400.00	$2,300.00	$2,100.00

Teddy™ the bear (R)
Cranberry, new face
Style #4052
Released: 1995

Born: n/a
Retired: 1995

Tag	S/1998	W/1998	S/1999
2nd	$2,000.00	$1,800.00	$1,800.00
3rd	$1,800.00	$1,650.00	$1,600.00

Teddy™ the bear (R)
Cranberry, old face
Style #4052
Released: 1994

Born: n/a
Retired: 1995

Tag	S/1998	W/1998	S/1999
1st	$2,400.00	$1,700.00	$1,800.00
2nd	$2,200.00	$1,600.00	$1,700.00

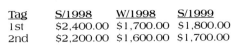

Teddy™ the bear (R)
Jade, new face
Style #4057
Released: 1995

Born: n/a
Retired: 1995

Tag	S/1998	W/1998	S/1999
2nd	$2,200.00	$1,900.00	$2,000.00
3rd	$1,900.00	$1,700.00	$1,800.00

Teddy™ the bear (R)
Jade, old face
Style #4057
Released: 1994

Born: n/a
Retired: 1995

Tag	S/1998	W/1998	S/1999
1st	$2,400.00	$1,800.00	$1,900.00
2nd	$2,200.00	$1,700.00	$1,800.00

Teddy™ the bear (R)
Magenta, new face
Style #4056
Released: 1995

Born: n/a
Retired: 1995

Tag	S/1998	W/1998	S/1999
2nd	$2,000.00	$1,900.00	$1,800.00
3rd	$2,000.00	$1,800.00	$1,700.00

Teddy™ the bear (R)
Magenta, old face
Style #4056
Released: 1994

Born: n/a
Retired: 1995

Tag	S/1998	W/1998	S/1999
1st	$2,100.00	$2,000.00	$1,800.00
2nd	$2,100.00	$1,800.00	$1,800.00

Teddy™ the bear (R)
Teal, new face
Style #4051
Released: 1995

Born: n/a
Retired: 1995

Tag	S/1998	W/1998	S/1999
2nd	$1,900.00	$2,100.00	$1,800.00
3rd	$1,900.00	$1,950.00	$1,800.00

Teddy™ the bear (R)
Teal, old face
Style #4051
Released: 1994

Born: n/a
Retired: 1995

Tag	S/1998	W/1998	S/1999
1st	$2,000.00	$1,800.00	$1,700.00
2nd	$2,000.00	$1,700.00	$1,700.00

Teddy™ the bear (R)
Violet, new face
Style #4055
Released: 1995

Born: n/a
Retired: 1995

Tag	S/1998	W/1998	S/1999
2nd	$2,200.00	$2,000.00	$1,800.00
3rd	$2,200.00	$1,800.00	$1,800.00

Teddy™ the bear (R)
Violet, old face
Style #4055
Released: 1994

Born: n/a
Retired: 1995

Tag	S/1998	W/1998	S/1999
1st	$2,200.00	$1,900.00	$1,900.00
2nd	$2,000.00	$1,700.00	$1,900.00

Tiny™ the chihuahua
Style #4234
Released: 12-31-98

Born: 9-8-98
Current

Tag	S/1999
5th	$8.00

Tiptoe™ the mouse
Style #4241
Released: 4-16-99

Born: 1-8-99
Current

Tag	S/1999
5th	$8.00

Tracker™ the basset hound
Style #4198
Released: 5-31-98

Born: 6-5-97
Current

Tag	W/1998	S/1999
5th	$10.00	$9.00

Trap™ the mouse (R)
Style #4042
Released: 1994

Born: n/a
Retired: 1995

Tag	S/1998	W/1998	S/1999
1st	$2,000.00	$1,700.00	$1,700.00
2nd	$1,700.00	$1,500.00	$1,550.00
3rd	$1,600.00	$1,300.00	$1,500.00

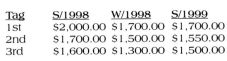

Tuffy™ the terrier (R)
Style #4108
Released: 5-11-97

Born: 10-12-96
Retired: 12-31-98

Tag	S/1998	W/1998	S/1999
4th	$10.00	$10.00	$10.00
5th	$8.00	$8.00	$9.00

Tusk™ the walrus (R)
Style #4076
Released: 1996
1st version: "Tuck" tags
2nd version: "Tusk" tags

Born: 9-18-95
Retired: 1-1-97

Ver.-Tag	S/1998	W/1998	S/1999
1st-3rd	$225.00	$175.00	$215.00
2nd-3rd	$200.00	$200.00	$170.00
2nd-4th	$200.00	$160.00	$140.00

Twigs™ the giraffe (R)
Style #4068
Released: 1996

Born: 5-19-95
Retired: 5-1-98

Ver.-Tag	S/1998	W/1998	S/1999
3rd	$115.00	$115.00	$95.00
4th	$10.00	$18.00	$15.00
5th	$9.00	$14.00	$15.00

Valentina™ the bear
Style #4233
Released: 12-31-98

Born: 2-14-98
Current

Tag	S/1999
5th	$9.00

Valentino™ the bear (R)
Style #4058
Released: 1995

Born: 2-14-94
Retired: 12-31-98

Ver.-Tag	S/1998	W/1998	S/1999
2nd	$350.00	$250.00	$240.00
3rd	$330.00	$200.00	$160.00
4th	$30.00	$22.00	$24.00
5th	$28.00	$18.00	$22.00

Velvet™ the panther (R)
Style #4064
Released: 1995

Born: 12-16-95
Retired: 9-30-97

Ver.-Tag	S/1998	W/1998	S/1999
3rd	$135.00	$100.00	$90.00
4th	$30.00	$30.00	$25.00

Waddle™ the penguin (R)
Style #4075
Released: 1995

Born: 12-19-95
Retired: 5-1-98

Ver.-Tag	S/1998	W/1998	S/1999
3rd	$120.00	$110.00	$100.00
4th	$12.00	$20.00	$18.00
5th	$12.00	$18.00	$18.00

Waves™ the whale (R)
Style #4084
Released: 5-11-97
1st version: "Echo" tags
2nd version: "Waves" tags

Born: 12-8-96
Retired: 5-1-98

Ver.-Tag	S/1998	W/1998	S/1999
1st-4th	$10.00	$15.00	$10.00
2nd-4th	$10.00	$13.00	$8.00
2nd-5th	$10.00	$12.00	$8.00

Web™ the spider (R)
Style #4041
Released: 1994

Born: n/a
Retired: 1995

Tag	S/1998	W/1998	S/1999
1st	$1,500.00	$1,700.00	$1,375.00
2nd	$1,400.00	$1,400.00	$1,300.00
3rd	$1,300.00	$1,200.00	$1,200.00

Weenie™ the dachshund (R)
Style #4013
Released: 1996

Born: 7-20-95
Retired: 5-1-98

Tag	S/1998	W/1998	S/1999
3rd	$115.00	$125.00	$115.00
4th	$15.00	$22.00	$25.00
5th	$16.00	$20.00	$24.00

Whisper™ the deer (R)
Style #4187
Released: 5-31-98

Born: 4-5-97
Current

Tag	W/1998	S/1999
5th	$12.00	$9.00

Wise™ the owl (R)
Style #4194
Released: 5-31-98

Born: 5-31-97
Retired: 12-31-98

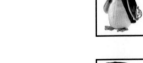

Tag	W/1998	S/1999
5th	$20.00	$14.00

Wiser™ the owl
Style #4238
Released: 4-22-99

Born: 6-4-99
Current

Tag	S/1999
5th	$9.00

Wrinkles™ the bulldog (R)
Style #4103
Released: 1996

Born: 5-1-96
Retired: 9-22-98

Tag	S/1998	W/1998	S/1999
4th	$11.00	$10.00	$11.00
5th	$8.00	$9.00	$9.00

Zero™ the penguin (R)
Style #4207
Released: 9-30-98

Born: 1-2-98
Retired: 12-31-98

Tag	S/1999
5th	$18.00

Ziggy™ the zebra (R)
Style #4063
Released: 1995

Born: 12-24-95
Retired: 5-1-98

Tag	S/1998	W/1998	S/1999
3rd	$115.00	$85.00	$75.00
4th	$15.00	$18.00	$15.00
5th	$14.00	$18.00	$12.00

Zip™ the cat (R)
Style #4004
Released: 1995

Born: 3-28-94
Retired: 5-1-98

1st version: white face and belly
2nd version: all black with pink ears
3rd version: white paws

Ver.-Tag	S/1998	W/1998	S/1999
1st-2nd	$625.00	$600.00	$500.00
1st-3rd	$475.00	$450.00	$450.00
2nd-3rd	$1,200.00	$1,450.00	$1,100.00
3rd-3rd	$175.00	$275.00	$200.00
3rd-4th	$25.00	$32.00	$24.00
3rd-5th	$22.00	$30.00	$22.00

New Releases

B.B. Bear the birthday bear
Style #4253
Released: 6-26-99

Born: n/a
Current

Flitter the Butterfly
Style #4255
Released: 6-26-99

Born: 6-2-99
Current

Lips the Fish
Style #4254
Released: 6-26-99

Born: 3-15-99
Current

Special Edition Beanie Babies®

Beanie Babies that commemorate special events such as Broadway shows or baseball games were very popular sellers at first, but have seen some decline in prices. Following the trend noted earlier in the book, people seem to be more interested in the Beanie itself, rather than the card or ribbon that comes with it. It's interesting to note that the more popular the Beanie and the team or Broadway show, the more popular each of these special edition Beanies.

★Beanie Baby® Official Club

Item	W/1998	S/1999
Clubby™	$50.00	$35.00
Clubby™ II	n/a	n/a

★Broadway Shows

Item	W/1998	S/1999
Candide		
Fleece™	$65.00	$20.00
Roary™	$60.00	$15.00
Fosse		
Scat™	n/a	$15.00
Strut®	$75.00	$25.00
Valentino™	n/a	$30.00
Joseph and the Amazing Technicolor Dreamcoat		
Fleece™	$40.00	$25.00
Garcia	$250.00	$200.00
Inch™	$50.00	$30.00
Peace™	$80.00	$30.00
Kiss of the Spider Woman		
Spinner™	n/a	$25.00
Livent		
Blackie™	n/a	$20.00
Hope™	n/a	$40.00
Loosy™	n/a	$15.00
Maple™	n/a	$200.00
Nanook™	$60.00	$25.00
Rocket™	n/a	$15.00
Music for All Tastes		
Fleece™	n/a	$20.00
Bongo™	n/a	$25.00
Oriental Theater (Chicago)		
Pugsly™	n/a	$25.00
Scorch™	n/a	$30.00
Phantom of the Opera		
Bongo™	$85.00	$55.00
Fortune™	n/a	$60.00
Gigi™	n/a	$40.00
Maple™	$375.00	$300.00
Peanut™	$90.00	$60.00
Velvet™	$80.00	$80.00
Ragtime		
Curly™ (burgundy, ivory, or navy ribbon), each	$60.00	$25.00
Glory™	n/a	$60.00
Nanook™ (burgundy, ivory, or navy ribbon), each	$45.00	$25.00
Signature Bear™ (burgundy or ivory), each	n/a	$50.00
Teddy™, NF brown	n/a	$175.00

Showboat

Goldie™	$70.00	$40.00
Peace™	$110.00	$35.00
Scoop™	$50.00	$20.00

Sunset Blvd.

Nuts™	n/a	$35.00

Sports Events
★Baseball

Item	W/1998	S/1999
1997		
Chicago Cubs, Cubbie™, 5-18-97	$210.00	$75.00
1998		
All Star Game, Glory™, 7-7-98	$240.00	$100.00
Anaheim Angels, Mel™, 9-6-98	n/a	$40.00
Arizona Diamondbacks, Hissy™, 6-14-98	$100.00	$35.00
Arizona Diamondbacks, Sly™, 8-27-98	n/a	$25.00
Atlanta Braves, Chip™, 8-19-98	$80.00	$40.00
Atlanta Braves, Pugsly™, 9-2-98	$70.00	$30.00
Chicago Cubs (a.k.a. "Harry Caray Daisy"), Daisy™, 5-3-98	$400.00	$200.00
Chicago Cubs, Gracie™, 9-13-98	$110.00	$60.00
Chicago Cubs Convention, Cubbie™	$400.00	$350.00
Chicago White Sox, Blizzard™, 7-12-98	$110.00	$65.00
Cincinnati Reds, Rover™, 8-16-98	$80.00	$45.00
Detroit Tigers, Stripes™, 5-31-98	$95.00	$45.00
Detroit Tigers, Stripes™, 8-8-98	$85.00	$45.00
Houston Astros, Derby™, 8-16-98	$100.00	$25.00
Kansas City Royals, Roary™, 5-31-98	$175.00	$40.00
Milwaukee Brewers, Batty™, 5-31-98	$100.00	$40.00
Minnesota Twins, Lucky™, 7-31-98	$75.00	$40.00
New York Mets, Batty™, 7-12-98	$60.00	$40.00
New York Mets, Curly™, 8-22-98	$70.00	$40.00
New York Yankees, Bones™, 3-10-98	n/a	$50.00
New York Yankees, Stretch™, 8-9-98	$90.00	$30.00
New York Yankees, Valentino™, 5-17-98	$220.00	$150.00
Oakland Athletics, Ears™, 3-15-98	$300.00	$75.00

Oakland Athletics, Peanut™, 8-1-98	$100.00	$35.00
Oakland Athletics, Peanut™, 9-6-98	n/a	$35.00
San Diego Padres, Waves™, 8-14-98	n/a	$40.00
San Francisco Giants, Tuffy™, 8-30-98	n/a	$25.00
St. Louis Cardinals, Smoochy™, 8-14-98	$75.00	$30.00
St. Louis Cardinals, Stretch™, 5-22-98	$140.00	$40.00
Seattle Mariners, Chocolate®, 9-5-98	n/a	$40.00
Tampa Bay Devil Rays, Pinky™, 8-23-98	n/a	$35.00
Tampa Bay Devil Rays, Weenie™, 6-26-98	$100.00	$35.00
Texas Rangers, Pugsly™, 8-4-98	n/a	$35.00
Toronto Blue Jays, Rocket™, 9-6-98	n/a	$40.00

1999

Arizona Diamondbacks, Goatee™, 7-8-99	n/a	n/a
Chicago Cubs Convention, Cubbie™	n/a	$175.00
Chicago Cubs, Erin™, 8-5-99	n/a	n/a
Chicago Cubs, Millenium™, 9-26-99	n/a	n/a
Chicago Cubs, Sammy™, 4-25-99	n/a	$65.00
Cincinnati Reds, Scorch™, 6-19-99	n/a	n/a
Detroit Tigers, Kuku™	n/a	n/a
Houston Astros, Tiny™, 7-18-99	n/a	n/a
Kansas City Royals, Fortune™, 6-6-99	n/a	n/a
Minnesota Twins, Hippie™, 6-18-99	n/a	n/a
Milwaukee Brewers, Robin™, 6-12-99	n/a	n/a
New York Mets, Valentina™	n/a	n/a
New York Yankees, Millenium™	n/a	n/a
New York Yankees, Signature Bear™	n/a	n/a
Oakland A's, Peace™, 5-1-99	n/a	n/a
St. Louis Cardinals, Mac™, 6-14-99	n/a	n/a
San Francisco Giants, Slippery™, 4-11-99	n/a	$25.00
Seattle Mariners, Batty™	n/a	n/a
Tampa Bay Devil Rays, Goochy™, 4-10-99	n/a	$30.00
Texas Rangers, Luke™	n/a	n/a

★Basketball (NBA)

Item	W/1998	S/1999
1998		
Cleveland Cavaliers, Bongo™, 4-5-98	$140.00	$45.00
Denver Nuggets, Chocolate®, 4-17-98	$80.00	$50.00
Indiana Pacers, Strut®, 4-2-98	$100.00	$40.00
Philadelphia 76ers, Baldy™, 1-17-98	$300.00	$40.00
San Antonio Spurs, Curly™, 4-27-98	$175.00	$60.00
San Antonio Spurs, Pinky™, 4-29-98	$150.00	$55.00

★Basketball (WNBA)

Item	W/1998	S/1999
1998		
Charlotte Sting, Curly™, 6-15-98	$300.00	$40.00
Cleveland Rockers, Curly™, 8-15-98	n/a	$35.00
Los Angeles Sparks, Mystic™, 8-3-98	n/a	$60.00
Washington Mystics, Mystic™, 7-11-98	$120.00	$55.00

★Football

Item	W/1998	S/1999
1998		
Blackie™, Chicago Bears Kids Club, 7-98	125.00	$25.00
Blackie™, Chicago Bears, 11-8-98	n/a	$35.00
Chocolate®, Dallas Cowboys, 9-6-98	n/a	$65.00
Chocolate®, Tennessee Oilers, 10-18-98	n/a	$30.00
Curly™, Chicago Bears, 12-20-98	n/a	$40.00
Derby™, Indianapolis Colts, 10-4-98	n/a	$30.00

★Hockey

Item	W/1998	S/1999
1998		
Boston Bruins, Blackie™, 10-12-98	n/a	$45.00
Buffalo Sabres, Spunky™, 10-23-98	n/a	$30.00
Chicago Blackhawks, Bones™, 10-24-98	n/a	$35.00
New Jersey Devils, Tuffy™, 10-24-98	n/a	$60.00
Phoenix Coyotes, Gobbles™, 11-26-98	n/a	$30.00
Pittsburgh Penguins, Waddle™, 10-24-98	n/a	$35.00
Pittsburgh Penguins, Waddle™, 11-21-98	n/a	$35.00
St. Louis Blues, Gobbles™, 11-24-98	n/a	$30.00

1999

Buffalo Sabres, Roam™, 2-19-99	n/a	$35.00
St. Louis Blues, Gobbles™, 3-22-99	n/a	$35.00
Toronto Maple Leafs, Chocolate®, 1-2-99	n/a	$45.00

★Miscellaneous

Item	W/1998	S/1999
#1 Bear™, Ty Representative Bear	n/a	$5,000.00
Billionaire Bear™, Ty Employee Bear	n/a	$3,000.00
Curly™, Toys for Tots, Fall 1998	n/a	$45.00
Maple™, Special Olympics	$425.00	$175.00
Teddy™, violet, NF, green bow, Ty Employee Bear	$3,500.00	$2,000.00
Teddy™, violet, NF, red bow, Ty Employee Bear	$3,500.00	$2,000.00
Valentino™, Special Olympics, July 1998	n/a	$60.00
Valentino™, Toys for Tots, March 1998	n/a	$50.00

Teenie Beanie Babies®

Mini versions of the big Beanie Babies, the Teenies are probably the all-time biggest fast-food promotion in history. Reportedly, 10 million of each of the 1997 characters were produced, and 20 million of each of the 1998 characters were made.

1997 Set (R)

Item	W/1998	S/1999
Complete 1997 set of 10, mint in bags	$150.00	$150.00
Chocolate® the moose, #4 of 10	$21.00	$16.00
Chops® the lamb, #3 of 10	$23.00	$12.00
Goldie™ the fish, #5 of 10	$12.00	$10.00
Lizz the lizard, #10 of 10	$13.00	$10.00
Patti® the platypus, #1 of 10	$26.00	$26.00
Pinky™ the flamingo, #2 of 10	$31.00	$28.00
Quacks™ the duck, #9 of 10	$11.00	$10.00
Seamore the seal, #7 of 10	$20.00	$17.00
Snort® the bull, #8 of 10	$11.00	$8.00
Speedy® the turtle, #6 of 10	$17.00	$15.00

1998 Set (R)

Item	W/1998	S/1999
Complete 1998 set of 12, mint in bags	$40.00	$30.00
Bones™ the dog, #9 of 12	$7.00	$4.00
Bongo™ the monkey, #2 of 12	$9.00	$7.00
Doby™ the doberman, #1 of 12	$8.00	$6.00
Happy™ the hippo, #6 of 12	$3.00	$2.00
Inch™ the inchworm, #4 of 12	$4.00	$2.00
Mel™ the koala, #7 of 12	$3.00	$3.00
Peanut™ the elephant, #12 of 12	$4.00	$3.00
Pinchers™ the lobster, #5 of 12	$3.00	$4.00
Scoop™ the pelican , #8 of 12	$3.00	$2.00
Twigs™ the giraffe, #3 of 12	$10.00	$12.00
Waddle™ the penguin, #11 of 12	$5.00	$3.00
Zip™ the cat, #10 of 12	$5.00	$3.00

1999 Set

Item	W/1998	S/1999
Complete 1999 set of 16, mint in bags	n/a	$50.00
Antsy™ the anteater	n/a	$2.00
Britannia™ the bear	n/a	$4.00
Chip™ the cat	n/a	$3.00
Claude™ the crab	n/a	$3.00
Erin™ the bear	n/a	$8.00
Freckles™ the leopard	n/a	$4.00
Glory™ the bear	n/a	$5.00
Iggy™ the iguana	n/a	$2.00
Maple™ the bear	n/a	$4.00
'Nook™ the husky	n/a	$2.00
Nuts™ the squirrel	n/a	$2.00
Rocket™ the blue jay	n/a	$2.00
Smoochy™ the frog	n/a	$2.00
Spunky™ the cocker spaniel	n/a	$3.00
Stretchy™ the ostrich	n/a	$2.00
Strut® the rooster	n/a	$2.00

Warner Brothers®
Studio Store Bean Bags

Warner Brothers Studio Store Bean Bags are hot items.
There are already many different versions of Scooby-Doo,
Taz, Tweety, and Bugs to collect. Along with Disney bean
bags and a few others, Warner's line has the greatest chance
to make a significant impact in the bean bag hobby in 1999
and beyond. Make sure you pick up holiday and other limited
edition bean bags, as these have proven very popular among
collectors. The Reindeer Scooby-Doo is the key to the set.
Check out http://www.bugsbeanies.com on the Internet—defi-
nitely your best bet for up-to-date information on this great
line of bean bags. You can also purchase the WB Bean Bags
online at: http://www.warnerbrothers.com

Tag Identification
Style 1 hang-tag (1997-1998)
The first hang-tags were big, and half dark and
half light. The name of the bean bag is not
included on the hang-tag.

Style 2 hang-tag (1998)
The second hang-tag was the same size as the
first, but all dark. The name of the bean bag is
not included on the hang-tag.

Style 3 hang-tag (1998)
The third hang-tag is smaller because, while it is
the same as the second style, the lower portion
that said "BEAN BAG" on the front and "CAR-
TOON NETWORK" on the back has been cut off.

Style 4 hang-tag (1998)
The fourth hang-tag is much smaller
and opens like a book. The inside of
the hang-tag has the name of the
bean bag.

Talking Bean Bags hang-tag
Medium-sized, with "SQUEEZE ME I TALK" on them. The bean bag's name is not on the tag.

Bath Floaters hang-tag
Medium-sized, red. The bean bag's name is not on the tag.

Special Tags
Christmas 1998 Gallery Event (U.K.), Halloween Tag 1998, Holiday 1997, Holiday 1998, Jack Frost Snowman, New York City Tag, *Quest for Camelot* Devon & Cornwall Tag.

Animaniacs®

Item	W/1998	S/1999
Dot (R)	$8.00	$8.00
Wakko (R)	$8.00	$8.00
Yakko (R)	$8.00	$8.00

Dot, Wakko, Yakko

Baby Looney Tunes®

Item	S/1999
Bugs	$7.00
Daffy	$7.00
Roadrunner	$7.00
Sylvester	$7.00
Taz	$7.00
Tweety	$7.00
Wile E. Coyote	$7.00

Front: Taz, Roadrunner, Sylvester, Tweety; Back: Daffy Duck, Wile E. Coyote, Bugs Bunny

Bath Floaters®

Item	W/1998	S/1999
Bugs Bunny	$8.00	$8.00
Scooby-Doo	$9.00	$8.00
Tweety	$8.00	$8.00

Bugs Bunny, Scooby-Doo, Tweety

Beaniture®

Item	S/1999
Orange Couch	$7.00
Purple Easy Chair	$6.00
Yellow Chair	$7.00
Table	n/a

Tweety in purple T-Shirt
on Purple Easy Chair

DC Comics®

Item	W/1998	S/1999
Aquaman	n/a	$7.00
Batgirl	n/a	$7.00
Batman	n/a	$7.00
Catwoman	n/a	$7.00
The Flash	n/a	$7.00
Harley Quinn	n/a	n/a
The Joker	n/a	n/a
Penguin	n/a	n/a
Poison Ivy	n/a	n/a
Riddler	n/a	n/a
Robin	n/a	$7.00
Space Ghost	n/a	$10.00
Superman	n/a	$7.00
Wonder Woman	n/a	$7.00

Front: Wonder Woman, Aquaman,
Superman, Green Lantern, Flash
Gordon; Back: Batman, Robin, Batgirl,
Catwoman

Space Ghost

Flintstones®

Item	W/1998	S/1999
Bamm Bamm	n/a	n/a
Barney	n/a	n/a
Betty	n/a	n/a
Dino (R)	$10.00	$9.00
Flintmobile, catalog/ QVC exclusive, 1999	n/a	n/a
Fred	n/a	n/a
The Great Gazoo, catalog/QVC exclusive, 1999	n/a	n/a
Pebbles	n/a	n/a
Wilma	n/a	n/a

Astro, Dino

Hanna-Barbera®

Item	W/1998	S/1999
Atom Ant	n/a	n/a
Augie Doggy (R)	n/a	$12.00
Baba Looey (R)	n/a	$8.00
Boo Boo	n/a	$11.00
Chopper (R)	n/a	$8.00
Dick Dastardly	n/a	n/a
Droopy	n/a	$7.00
Dum Dum (R)	n/a	$8.00
Frankenstein Jr.	n/a	n/a
Hardy Har Har (R)	n/a	$8.00
Hong Kong Phooey (R)	$8.00	$10.00
Huckleberry Hound (R)	n/a	$8.00
Jabber Jaw	n/a	n/a
Jerry	$8.00	$7.00
Magilla Gorilla	n/a	n/a
Morocco Mole (R)	n/a	$8.00
Mutley	$8.00	$7.00
Penelope Pitstop	n/a	n/a
Quick Draw McGraw	n/a	$7.00
Ranger Smith	n/a	$7.00
Secret Squirrel	n/a	n/a
Snagglepuss (R)	n/a	$10.00
Space Ghost (R)	n/a	$10.00
Speed Buggy (R)	n/a	$9.00
Squiddly-Diddly (R)	n/a	$8.00
The Wolf	n/a	n/a
Tom	$8.00	$7.00
Top Cat	n/a	n/a
Touche Turtle (R)	n/a	$8.00
Yakky Doodle (R)	n/a	$8.00
Yogi Bear	n/a	$7.00

Tom, Jerry

Front: Quick Draw McGraw, Yakky Doodle, Snagglepuss, Touche Turtle; Back: Speed Buggy, Mutley

Front: Augie Doggie, Huckleberry Hound, Hong Kong Phooey; Back: Dum Dum, Boo Boo, Droopy

The Jetsons®

Item	W/1998	S/1999
Astro (R)	$10.00	$10.00
Elroy	n/a	$7.00
George	n/a	$7.00
Jane	n/a	$7.00
Judy	n/a	$7.00
Rosie the Robot	n/a	$7.00

The King and I®

Item	S/1999
Anna (R)	$7.00
The King (R)	$7.00
The Kralahome (R)	$7.00
Master Little (R)	$7.00
Moonshee the Monkey (R)	$7.00
The Prince (R)	$7.00
Princess Ying (R)	$7.00
Rama the Panther (R)	$7.00
Tuptim (R)	$7.00
Tusker the Elephant (R)	$7.00

The King, Anna

Moonshee the Monkey, The Kralahome

Looney Tunes®

Item	W/1998	S/1999
Bugs Bunny (V1: bigger)	$10.00	$10.00
Bugs Bunny (V2: smaller)	$8.00	$7.00
Bugs Bunny, Birthday	n/a	$7.00
Bugs Bunny, Carrot, Easter 1999 (R)	n/a	$8.00
Bugs Bunny, Christmas 1999, musical	n/a	n/a
Bugs Bunny, Easter, 1998 (R)	$38.00	$14.00
Bugs Bunny, Hawaii, 1999, Hawaii exclusive	n/a	$10.00
Bugs Bunny, Liberty, New York exclusive	n/a	$9.00

Bugs Bunny Birthday, Sylvester Birthday

Bugs Bunny—Front: Easter, w/Carrot 1998, Rabbit Season, Snowman; Back: V1, V2

Bugs Bunny, Millooneyum	n/a	n/a
Bugs Bunny, Musical Xmas 1999	n/a	n/a
Bugs Bunny, Rabbit Season (R)	n/a	$8.00
Bugs Bunny, Snowman, 1998 (R)	n/a	$10.00
Bugs Bunny, Snowman, 1998, extra UK tag (R)	n/a	$40.00
Bugs Bunny, Stars & Stripes, 1999 (R)	n/a	n/a
Bugs Bunny, Talking	$11.00	$10.00
Bugs Bunny, Trick or Treat, catalog/QVC exclusive	n/a	n/a
Bugs Bunny, with carrot, catalog exclusive, 1998 (R)	$25.00	$15.00

Commander K-9 (R) $8.00		$10.00
Commander K-9, Reindeer, 1998 (R) $12.00		$10.00

Front: Marvin, Marvin Santa;
Back: Commander K-9,
Commander K-9 Reindeer

Front: Foghorn Leghorn,
Marc Antony, Henery Hawk,
Gossamer; Back: Michigan J.
Frog, Daffy Duck, Daffy Duck
Season

Daffy Duck	$8.00	$7.00
Daffy Duck, Duck Season (R)	n/a	$8.00
Daffy Duck, Talking	n/a	$10.00
Duck Dodgers	n/a	n/a
Elmer Fudd	n/a	n/a
Foghorn Leghorn (R)	$9.00	$8.00
Foghorn Leghorn, Talking	n/a	n/a
Gossamer (R)	$9.00	$10.00
Henery Hawk (R)	$8.00	$8.00
Lola Bunny	n/a	$7.00
Marc Antony (R)	$8.00	$9.00
Marvin the Martian (R)	$8.00	$10.00
Marvin the Martian, Santa, 1998 (R)	$12.00	$10.00
Marvin the Martian, Millooneyum	n/a	n/a
Michigan J. Frog (R)	$9.00	$9.00
Michigan J. Frog, Talking	n/a	$12.00
Penelope	$8.00	$7.00

Penelope, Bride	n/a	$10.00
Pepe LePew	$10.00	$7.00
Pepe LePew, Groom	n/a	$10.00
Pepe LePew, Prisoner of Love(R)	n/a	$9.00
Petunia Pig (R)	$8.00	$9.00
Porky Pig (R)	$8.00	$8.00
Porky Pig, Talking	n/a	$12.00
Pussyfoot (R)	$9.00	$9.00
Roadrunner	$10.00	$8.00
Roadrunner, Talking	n/a	n/a
She-Devil (R)	n/a	$8.00
Speedy Gonzalez (V1: black tail and fuzzy hair) (R)	$8.00	$8.00
Speedy Gonzalez (V2: brown tail and felt hair) (R)	n/a	$8.00
Speedy Gonzalez, Feliz Navidad	n/a	n/a
Speedy Gonzalez, Talking	n/a	$12.00
Sylvester	$8.00	$7.00
Sylvester, Birthday	n/a	$8.00
Sylvester, Halloween	n/a	n/a
Sylvester, Millooneyum	n/a	n/a
Sylvester, Pilgrim	n/a	n/a
Sylvester, Santa, catalog/QVC exclusive, 1998 (R)	$14.00	$10.00
Sylvester, Talking	n/a	n/a
Taz	$8.00	$7.00
Taz, Birthday (R)	$11.00	$8.00
Taz, Devil	$12.00	$22.00
Taz, Harley	n/a	n/a
Taz, Millooneyum	n/a	n/a
Taz, Motorcycle	n/a	$8.00
Taz, Stocking, 1998 (R)	$12.00	$9.00
Taz, Superman	n/a	n/a
Taz, Talking	$11.00	$10.00
Taz, Xmas 1999	n/a	n/a
Tweety	$8.00	$7.00
Tweety, 1999 date	n/a	$10.00
Tweety, bath floater	$8.00	$8.00
Tweety, Birthday, 1st: yellow/blue hat (R)	$11.00	$9.00

Front: Yosemite Sam, Penelope, Speedy Gonzalez V1; Back: Sylvester, Sylvester Santa, Wile E. Coyote, Roadrunner

Tweety—Front: Pumpkin, Nightshirt, Cute, 1999, Sweet; Back: New York, Tweety, Birthday (Green/Blue), Birthday (Yellow/Blue, Santa)

Item		
Tweety, Birthday, 2nd: green/blue hat (R)	$11.00	$9.00
Tweety, Cupid, 1998 (R)	n/a	$12.00
Tweety, Cute	n/a	$8.00
Tweety, Easter Rabbit, 1999 (R)	n/a	$11.00
Tweety, Graduate (R)	n/a	$10.00
Tweety, Hanukkah	n/a	n/a
Tweety, Heart, catalog/ QVC exclusive (R)	n/a	$24.00
Tweety, Indian	n/a	n/a
Tweety, It's a Girl	n/a	$9.00
Tweety, Millooneyum	n/a	n/a
Tweety, New York (a.k.a. Liberty), NY exclusive	$35.00	$11.00
Tweety, Nightshirt (R)	$9.00	$9.00
Tweety, Pink Rose, catalog/QVC exclusive	n/a	$10.00
Tweety, Pumpkin, 1998 (R)	$12.00	$18.00
Tweety, Purple T-shirt	n/a	$7.00
Tweety, Roman, Las Vegas exclusive	n/a	$10.00
Tweety, St. Patrick's Day, 1999 (R)	n/a	$15.00
Tweety, Santa, LE 1998 (R)	$12.00	$12.00
Tweety, Skeleton	n/a	n/a
Tweety, Sweet (a.k.a. Mother's Day), 1998 (R)	$11.00	$10.00
Tweety, T-shirt (Beverly Hills)	n/a	n/a
Tweety, T-shirt (Boston)	n/a	n/a
Tweety, T-shirt (Hawaii)	n/a	$10.00
Tweety, T-shirt (Las Vegas)	n/a	$10.00
Tweety, T-shirt (Maui)	n/a	n/a
Tweety, T-shirt (New York)	n/a	$10.00
Tweety, T-shirt (San Francisco)	n/a	$15.00
Tweety, Talking	$11.00	$10.00
Tweety, Xmas 1999	n/a	n/a
Wile E. Coyote	$9.00	$9.00
Yosemite Sam	$9.00	$9.00
Yosemite Sam, Talking	n/a	$9.00

Movie Limited Editions

Item	W/1998	S/1999
Bladebeak (R)	n/a	$7.00
Devon & Cornwall (R)	$12.00	$9.00
Gizmo	n/a	n/a
Iron Giant	n/a	n/a
Jack Frost (R)	n/a	$9.00

Devon & Cornwall,
Bladebeak, Jack Frost

Pinky and the Brain®

Item	W/1998	S/1999
Brain	$9.00	$8.00
Brain, Xmas 1998 (R)	n/a	$10.00
Pinky	$9.00	$8.00
Pinky, Xmas (R)	n/a	$10.00

Front: Pinky, Brain; Back:
Pinky Xmas, Brain Xmas

Scooby-Doo®

Item	W/1998	S/1999
Daphne	n/a	$7.00
Fred	n/a	$7.00
Scooby-Doo (V1: "S" on collar)	$12.00	$27.00
Scooby-Doo (V2: "SD" on collar)	$8.00	$8.00
Scooby-Doo, Antlers, 1998 (R)	$12.00	$13.00
Scooby-Doo, Baseball (V1: no freckles on chin, Father's Day) (R)	$13.00	$10.00
Scooby-Doo, Baseball (V2: freckles on chin, Father's Day) (R)	$12.00	$10.00
Scooby-Doo, bath floater	$9.00	$10.00
Scooby-Doo, Birthday	n/a	$10.00
Scooby-Doo, Graduate (R)	n/a	$15.00
Scooby-Doo, Easter 1998 (R)	$65.00	$40.00
Scooby-Doo, Easter 1999 (R)	n/a	$10.00
Scooby-Doo, Hawaii, Hawaii exclusive	n/a	$20.00
Scooby-Doo, Home Run	n/a	$10.00
Scooby-Doo, I Love New York, NY exclusive	$16.00	$12.00
Scooby-Doo, It's a Boy	n/a	$12.00
Scooby-Doo, Nutcracker, 1998 (R)	$12.00	$10.00
Scooby-Doo, Pilgrim	n/a	n/a
Scooby-Doo, Reindeer, 1997 (R)	$225.00	$175.00
Scooby-Doo, Roman, Las Vegas exclusive	n/a	$13.00
Scooby-Doo, Snowman	n/a	n/a
Scooby-Doo, Surfboard	n/a	$8.00
Scooby-Doo, T-shirt (Atlantic City)	n/a	$18.00

Scooby-Doo, T-shirt (Chicago)	n/a	$20.00
Scooby-Doo, T-shirt (Lake Tahoe)	n/a	n/a
Scooby-Doo, Talking	$14.00	$12.00
Scooby-Doo, Vampire, 1998 (R)	$12.00	$15.00
Scooby-Doo, Witch	n/a	n/a
Scooby-Doo, Xmas 1999	n/a	n/a
Scooby-Doo, Year 2000	n/a	n/a
Scrappy	n/a	$8.00
Shaggy	n/a	$7.00
Velma	n/a	$7.00

Scooby-Doo—Front: Baseball V1, Baseball V2; Back: V1, V2, I Love NY

Scooby-Doo—I Love NY, Home Run, Surfboard

Scooby-Doo—Front: Easter 1998, Reindeer; Back: Antlers, Nutcracker, Vampire

Wizard of Oz®

Item	W/1998	S/1999
Cowardly Lion	n/a	$10.00
Dorothy	n/a	$10.00
Flying Monkey	n/a	$10.00
Glinda	n/a	$10.00
Lollipop Boy	n/a	$10.00
Lollipop Girl	n/a	$10.00
Scarecrow	n/a	$10.00
Tin Man	n/a	$12.00
Toto	n/a	$12.00
Wicked Witch	n/a	$10.00
Wizard	n/a	$10.00

Front: Flying Monkey, Glinda, Wizard, Dorothy, Lollipop Boy, Lollipop Girl; Back: Wicked Witch, Tin Man, Scarecrow, Lion, Toto

Index

About the Author

Shawn Brecka is long-time antiques and collectibles enthusiast and the author of three books: *The Bean Family Album*, *The Bean Family Pocket Guide*, and *Collecting in Cyberspace*. She's the editor-at-large for *Beans & Bears!* magazine, and her articles on bean bags have appeared in the *Antique Trader Weekly* and *Toy Trader*. In addition, she enjoys surfing the Internet, searching for bean bag plush, and adding to her other collections of ruby red glass, vintage purses, beaded collars, and sewing items.